THE BLUE WINGS

of the

DRAGONFLY

FINDING MAGIC IN EVERY DAY, EVERYONE, AND EVERYTHING

BY C. LEE ROGGEMAN

C. Lee Roggeman

**The Blue Wings of The Dragonfly,
Finding Magic in Everyday, Everyone,
and Everything**

**Copyright © 2018 by C. Lee Roggeman aka
Cynthia Roggeman**

All rights reserved.

Book design by C. Lee Roggeman

Front and Back Cover Image: © Fiametta Segatori

Back Page Author Image and Dragonfly Watercolor in Book:
© Heather MacKenzie

Dragonflies Sketches between chapters: © Karamfila,
Licensed through Creative Market

Visit my website at www.CLeeRoggeman.com

Printed in the United States of America

First Printing April 2018

Published by: Sojourn Publishing, LLC

Paperback ISBN: 978-1-62747-254-8

Ebook ISBN: 978-1-62747-256-2

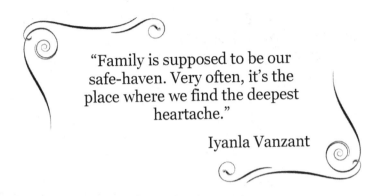

"Family is supposed to be our safe-haven. Very often, it's the place where we find the deepest heartache."

Iyanla Vanzant

DEDICATION

I dedicate this book first to my family because they are the cornerstone; without their influences, my perceptions and abilities to cope would be altered. The family is where we learn our core existence. We can have love-hate relationships or unconditional love.

It is a bond that will never be completely broken. Energies are connected. Hearts are in tune. They are the people we have known the longest on this Earth plane. Though wounded at times, we always survive, each time with more understanding. I love the family that was chosen for me. No one is perfect, but I accept them and myself for who we are, all on different paths and journeys but joined by fate.

To all the families who have dealt with alcoholism, bi-polar disorder, depression, dysfunction, loss and love, I wish you peace in the silence.

Thankful for:

Some of my dear friends who believed in me and were supportive in the writing of this book. They provided some needed technical support and supportive thoughts in the preparation of, this book. I am grateful to have them in my life.

Briana Berryman

Lu Sevigny

Tammy Franco

Carol Bailin

Catherine Yunt

Special Endorsements and Acknowledgements

The Blue Wings of the Dragonfly is a heartfelt tale of triumph and tragedy, of being tested by the universe over and over. In reading it, you'll feel as though you're simply having a conversation with the author, one in which she takes you into the most personal aspects of her life. It tugs at your heartstrings, and you'll likely find yourself tearing up – but ultimately leaving with a feeling of hope for yourself and this life.

Chelsea Young, Editor-in-Chief of So Scottsdale! Magazine and Author of the forthcoming children's book, The Color of Mother.

The Blue Wings of the Dragonfly is an inspiring biographical tale of a survivor. This woman's life journey has been riddled with unforeseen circumstances which she learned how to overcome on her own and now shares with us. This book is truly a lesson in how to summon our strength to conquer anything we face externally or internally as we walk this earth. I can honestly say I am a better person with more insight and wisdom to cope with life after having read this book.

Jaime Abromovitz, Best Selling Dreamalings Series Children's Book Author and Best Selling Songwriter and Lyricist.

This manuscript is quite powerful, with some heartrending sadness, usually followed with joy – and then deep introspection about how life often works that way.

I liked it very much; there are two sections that felt like a stab in the heart: the first when the author was virtually forced by her father to undergo an abortion; the second when the author had to have Jazz, her dog, put down. There is no way a reader can avoid being deeply touched by these moments – and others like it that occur throughout this manuscript.

Bill Worth—Editor, and Author of the novels "House of the Sun: A Metaphysical Novel of Maui," and "The Hidden Life of Jesus Christ: A Memoir," and the newly published non-fiction book exploring his 28 - year journey with multiple sclerosis: "Outwitting Multiple Sclerosis: How forgiveness Helped Me Heal My Brain By Changing My Mind."

In this all too human memoir, you'll walk casually through childhood moments and adult routines periodically seized with fear, shame, anger and deep loss as you journey through Roggeman's world. Veiled thinly beneath the graceful and sweet storyline is everyone's journey through life. Messy, absurd and overflowing with affliction and loss. It speaks to us of being human through pain, yet always alluding to change, growth and hope. Moving and tender, you're compelled towards unity and possibility as you cry and smile with her.

Jim Spina, Nuclear Physicist, Author of the soon to be released book, I Almost Murdered a Complete Stranger.

CONTENTS

NOTES FROM THE AUTHOR

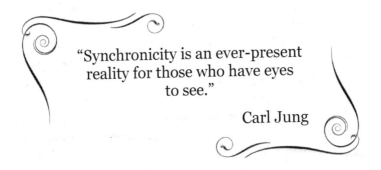

"Synchronicity is an ever-present reality for those who have eyes to see."

Carl Jung

Perhaps I should tell you how this journey began, culminating with the book you're holding in your hands right now. The writing of this book, the words on paper, was brought about by a series of events and synchronicities the likes of which I had never seen. Many of the events were experienced as crisis and trauma and were exceedingly painful. More importantly, they ultimately served as healing from within.

We don't realize all the things we internalize. They dwell in the shadows of our mind until a light shines on them. Suddenly we're able to process and integrate all that we have learned about ourselves over the years. The true nature of one's self is amazing, far beyond our self- image. Understanding the why, the purpose and meaning behind them, is incredible. The ability to forgive not only myself, but others who have touched my life if only to allow me a glimpse of who I am, or who I came to be resulting from the life I have lived and the experiences I have had is profound.

I received an email for a writing retreat so, I sent it to my brother Jim. He called and said, "Let's do this!" He booked his flight into Arizona for March 1, 2017, and we were on the road to Sedona the next day. We were both going through our traumas, still sick and healing, but for some reason, we knew this was the right thing to do. We have always journaled; he is retired now, and I'm not working. The odds of this all lining up were crazy! Somehow, as tired and ill as we both were, we made it through. We have written our books. There has been a wonderful camaraderie between us in sharing our stories and childhood memories from different perspectives.

The healing that has taken place within me as I write is amazing, as I am releasing old wounds that were buried very deep inside me for a long time. I am surrendering and letting go of them, one by one. Some are childhood-related, while others are from trauma: the loss of people I love, a dear pet is gone, and illness. It's helped me to open my heart, to hear a new song if I listen quietly enough. I can hear my heart sing in the quietness; the sound of silence has become my ally.

This book is about loving who you are, giving back to society and embracing your fears. It takes courage not to be afraid of revealing, or feeling your hidden emotions. Your Vulnerability can be a tool for survival to weather the storm of life. It is about family, abandonment, the complexity, and frailty of the human body, the revival of the human spirit, coping mechanisms, overcoming adversity, finding your identity after loss and joy after trauma, grieving and sadness.

Compelling and written from the heart. By chance, I think not. Everything happens for a reason. We may not recognize it at the time, but the reason will eventually be revealed. I learned to be the dutiful daughter, the caring mother, the loving wife, and the devoted sibling. Somewhere in all of this, I lost myself along the way. I hope that this book will help others find themselves. To have a better understanding of life and what makes you happy, sad, joyful, fearful and loved. To follow your inner guidance to listen and know that in the silence is where you will find yourself, for you are never alone. It's important that you discover your BLISS!

INTRODUCTION

My memoir, the sharing of some of my life stories that weave together the interconnectedness and synchronicities of all people and events in my life. As life unfolds, it allows us to realize that we are all divinely led. Coincidences? I think not! There is a purpose in everything. We are never alone. Our experiences, both good and bad, leave us with a spiritual understanding of life and death, the reason for our being.

You are strong, courageous and capable. You have potential, talents, gifts, astonishing qualities, and joy to spread that will change people regardless of who you think you are. A man, a woman, who loves, encourages, comforts, shares and teaches. We can all bring change to our shattered world. Surrender to the process and remember the importance of gratitude.

YOU are AMAZING!

ADVICE FROM A DRAGONFLY:

SPEND TIME NEAR THE WATER

BE COLORFUL

ENJOY A GOOD REED

ZOOM IN ON YOUR DREAMS

APPRECIATE LONG SUMMER DAYS

KEEP YOUR EYES OPEN

JUST WING IT

Ilan Shamir

SCIENCE NEWS
Magazine issue: Vol. 191, No. 13, July 8, 2017, p.4

The blue wings of this dragonfly may be surprisingly alive

An adult insect wing is basically dead.

So, what in the world were tiny respiratory channels doing in a wing membrane of a morpho dragonfly?

Rhainer Guillermo Ferreira was so jolted by a scanning electron microscope image showing what looked like skinny, branching tracheal tubes in a morpho wing that he called in another entomologist for a second opinion. Guillermo Ferreira, then at Kiel University in Germany, showed the image to a colleague who also was "shocked," he remembers. A third entomologist was called in. There was shock all around.

The shimmering, sky blue wings of male Zenithoptera dragonflies might be unexpectedly and fully alive, Guillermo Ferreira says. That bold idea will take some testing. So, for now, he and colleagues report the unusual tracheal respiratory system, the first in any insect wing as far as they know, in the May Biology Letters.

Wings of insects start as living tissue, but as the creatures take their adult form, cells die between the strut work of supporting wing veins. The dried-out zones can go cellophane-clear or cover themselves in color, bordered by the vein network like the glass pieces in a cathedral window. The veins, as they are called, have their own respiratory tubes, nerves and such. But entomologists thought the rest of the insect wing would be no more alive and in need of oxygen than toenail clippings. Living, breathing, wings might help explain how South America's four or five species of morpho dragonflies make such complicated blue color, says Guillermo Ferreira, now at the Federal University of Sao Carlos in Brazil. Blue pigment, rare in nature, is nowhere on these wings. Instead, the wings, perhaps powered by abundant oxygen, create a living layer cake of light-manipulating doodads.

In the tough inner layers, male Z. lanei wings form nanoscale spheres sandwiched between blankets of black pigment-filled nanolayers. This setup can enhance reflections of blue light and muddle other wavelengths. On top are two more light-trick layers, each made of wax crystals. The uppermost crystals, Guillermo Ferreira found, are shaped "like little leaves."

Better blues might help a male intimidate rivals for breeding territory around the edges of their palm tree swamp homeland. Male dragonflies don't just dart and bluff. Guillermo Ferreira often sees a male "rushing toward the rival, grabbing the wings, biting the wings and then sometimes biting the head."

In spite of the world-class color nanogadgetry, males aren't known for courtship displays, he says. "The female just flies in, and he just grabs her."

This story was updated July 17, 2017, to correct the video credit.

INVICTUS
By William Ernest Henley

Out of the night that covers me
Black as the pit from pole to pole,
I thank whatever gods may be
For my unconquerable soul.

In the fell clutch of circumstance
I have not winced nor cried aloud.
Under the bludgeonings of chance
My head is bloody but unbowed.

Beyond this place of wrath and tears
Looms but the Horror of the shade,
And yet the menace of the years
Finds and shall find me unafraid.

It matters not how strait the gate,
How charged with punishments the scroll,
I am the master of my fate,
I am the captain of my soul.

Invictus is my favorite poem about
displaying fortitude in the face of adversity.

MAY YOU TOUCH DRAGONFLIES AND TALK TO THE MOON

BOOM, CRASH

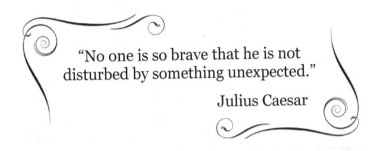

"No one is so brave that he is not
disturbed by something unexpected."

Julius Caesar

The beginning, how it all started. It was a beautiful
Friday afternoon on October 16, 2015. I had just
gotten off work, and some light rain had fallen that
day. As I was driving, the sun came out, and this
gorgeous double rainbow was right in front of me.
I was gazing at it, sitting at a red light when
BOOM! I was thrown forward and wasn't sure at
first what had happened. A man in a truck behind
me was getting out of his vehicle, profusely
apologizing for hitting me and saying he didn't see
the red light, later admitting he was texting.

My phone had flown out of the window from my
console, although I didn't know it until we pulled
over to the side. I was searching under the seats and
mats, frantic at this point; then I looked over and
there it was in the middle of the road, smashed to
pieces. My heart sunk as I ran, to pick it up. There
was nothing, no signal. My neck was hurting, a
headache starting, we exchanged information. I

needed to get to the Verizon store before they closed, as this was my only phone.

After waiting for two hours, the phone that they could give me was a flip phone, until the one I had on order came in. That first night was unnerving. I was not feeling well and spent a lot of time that night, glancing at my nightstand, looking for the all too familiar green light on the top of my phone and realizing it wasn't there. Funny how something as simple as a little green light could bring comfort and connectedness to the outside world. I was not even sure I could see to dial out for an emergency on the temporary cell phone.

I saw my primary care physician on the following Monday; he ordered physical therapy for my whiplash. An appointment with my spine surgeon is also scheduled to make sure that a previous injury to my C-5 and C-6 vertebrae, had not been refractured. The spine surgeon orders a myelogram. A test in which the doctor inserts a hollow needle through your skin into the spinal canal. The dye is then injected into the space surrounding the spinal cord and nerve roots. This dye is radiopaque, meaning it's impenetrable by x-ray. Then x-rays and a CT scan are done. The procedure is quite painful, and you have to lie perfectly still for the duration. Upon leaving I am given instructions to remain at a 45-degree angle for the next 48 hours so the injection site can close properly. My entire body is hurting. A couple of days later the surgeon advises that the films look good no new fractures were seen. I keep complaining to my endodontist that it hurts when I bite down on the lower right-hand side of my mouth. He takes X-rays; nothing shows up. Then, a few months later, a fracture shows up under the crown. The tooth would have to be extracted, and an implant put in. It is July 18, 2016. When I arrive at the dental office, there seems to be some confusion. My periodontist, whom I had met and spoken with, is no longer working for this organization. Another doctor has been brought in to do this procedure. They are late getting started, and he doesn't seem to be happy about the whole situation. (Which, by the way, is not making me feel all warm and fuzzy). He proceeds to start injecting the Lidocaine; it is my first time for this.

I have always been able to do self-hypnosis at the dentist without the use of anesthesia, but this is surgery. After many attempts and numerous shots, he cannot get the tooth out. It fractures, and I tell him it's throbbing. I can feel what he is doing. Frustrated, he throws his hands in the air and leaves the room to get my endodontist. My body is now shaking from all the pain.

The endodontist comes in and calmly sits down beside me. "It's okay," he says. "Tell me what's wrong." I relay everything back to him, and he tells me he's going to do a pain block for me, and then the periodontist will finish. The pain block is administered. I slowly stop shivering, and the throbbing ceases. My body relaxes again; he squeezes my shoulder and exits the room. The surgeon returns, the extraction is done, and a bone graft is put in to help support a titanium post that will be put in three months later.

Not long after, on August 6, 2016, I received an alarming phone call: my brother has been Airvac'd to a hospital in Maryland, and he was not expected to live. Constant phone calls and texts with his wife. He finally came out of a coma after three weeks, facing a long road to recovery. I'm grateful he made it through this ordeal.

In October, I lost my job due to so many days off work since the accident. So I decided to start looking after the implant was completed. On, November 11, 2016, the titanium post is put in for my implant, and the doctor punctures the lingual plate in the process. He should have known immediately; however, he does not. I end up spending the entire next year suffering from illness and eight surgeries all because of the ineptness of a doctor.

Life is so fragile it can crumble in an instant. We never know what life is going to bring us. It is full of surprises and twists and turns, but there is a plan unfolding; many times, one we may not have chosen, at least not that we can remember. It is out of our control. Surrender to the divine. There is always a silver lining.

A BRUSH WITH MORTALITY

*"Suddenly you just know it's time
to start something new and trust the
magic of new beginnings."*

Unknown

Walking into the emergency room, the girl behind the admittance desk takes one look at me, and I can see she is trying to keep from staring. The right side of my face is extremely swollen. The infection is heading up to my temporal lobe. I am unrecognizable to anyone who knows me. The pain is excruciating.

As I'm answering questions, time seems as though it is standing still. A plastic arm bracelet is put on my left wrist. I'm then taken to an ER room, and they start drawing blood and running vitals. The doctor who comes in is part of a myofascial surgical team they have on staff. He informs me that I need surgery as soon as possible. I am put in a type of pod room and given a blue hospital gown to wear.

The room is cold. I'm shivering. The nurse brings me some warm blankets, and they are momentarily comforting. The blood work comes back; unfortunately, my potassium and magnesium levels are so low from trying to fight the infection for the last five days, that it would put me at risk for a heart attack. I think, is this happening. I have only been in a hospital once before. I am scared. My son David and daughter-in-law Nicole arrive; for a while, I am calmer.

The night nurse comes in and introduces himself, giving me one of many doses of potassium to drink during the night. I am hooked up to the IV saline and antibiotic drip bags. I hate needles in my arm. It hurts. No hospital rooms were available, so that first night I spent in the ER pod room. The ER is noisy, so many disturbances its constant pandemonium there is no peace to be found anywhere even behind the closed curtain. You can hear beeping sounds from all directions, different codes called over the loudspeaker, people scattering everywhere, the sounds of illness and trauma.

The antibiotics started making me sick to my stomach. All night, I had to endure going down the hall to a shared restroom tethered to my IV pole, which I decided to call R2D2 because he seems to be the only one I can talk to and is a constant companion for what turns out to be a two-week stay in the hospital. It was awful. There was an elderly gentleman who I would see headed to the restroom as he passed my pod, and I quickly learned to get up and beat him there because he would piss all over the bathroom floor and the socks they give you to wear would get sticky on the bottom from his mess. The nurse finally brought me about eight pairs, bless her soul. How could I be so OCD and on death's door at the same time? I didn't think I would make it through the night.

On November 24, 2016, at 7:00 the next morning, I was taken into surgery. My anxiety was off the charts, but I was so sick that anything seemed better than what I was experiencing. After waking up in the recovery room and pain medicine was administered to keep me comfortable, they informed me they had a room and bed available. My face and mouth were so bruised and swollen. There were ridges on the inside of my right cheek from being irrigated, a drain tube coming out under my chin, and what I would refer to as "the sinkhole" where they had removed the titanium post for an implant. I could hardly open my mouth to get liquids down. Antibiotics and pain medication were wreaking havoc on my stomach. The hospital gown was ridiculous. It felt like a huge tent on me and kept falling off my shoulders everytime I moved.

The surgeon arrived later that day; he informed me that my lingual plate was pierced or punctured when the titanium post was put in, creating a crevice for bacteria to grow and spread like wildfire throughout my face and jaw. If I had waited another 24 hours to come in, I might not be here today. I was stressed and depressed; it was Thanksgiving Day and instead of getting to spend it with my family, I was alone and in the hospital. The day was redeemed later when my son David and daughter-in-law Nicole brought my two grandchildren to see me. My grandson, who was six at the time, looked at me and said, "Nana you look weird." It was the first time I had laughed in a while. He then proceeded to come and sit by me playing with his iPad like nothing was different. My granddaughter hid behind the safety of her dad, not liking it when someone is ill. I like to think of her as a very sensitive child, not wanting to see someone in pain. Still, it was good to see them.

The hospital was built in 1978, and it consisted of a monolithic concrete bed tower designed in shell form. The windows are oval shaped, and the hospital itself looks like something you would see on the old cartoon series "The Jetsons." Staring out my hospital window as night falls, I watch as the city lights begin to illuminate the landscape. There is life outside of these walls, I think. There are other human beings; other human beings all going through their drama and joys. I remember a quote by Henry David Thoreau, from the book "Walden." "Most men lead lives of quiet desperation." Somehow it made me feel less sad and anxious, giving me hope for another day.

On November 26, 2016, at 5:30 a.m., when the room's lights wake me from a sound sleep, the doctors inform me that I will have to go back in for more surgery. They are having a hard time getting ahead of the infection. I'm not allowed any food or water while waiting on an operating room to become available that day. The orderly comes to wheel me down the now familiar hallways. Back into surgery, I'm again wondering if I will wake up and make it through all of this.

My eyes open. I am in recovery again. Somewhere inside, a smile resides. I am in severe pain, and the nurse starts to administer medicine until I can tell him that I am comfortable. I have no sense of time. I am brought back to my room by the orderly. I find myself pondering anesthesia, a state of temporary induced loss of sensation or awareness. Does the mind just shut down temporarily? And how do we come back with no memory of what went on while under its effects? It is still a mystery to me.

Later that day, an infectious disease doctor, who had been handling my antibiotics, enters my room and introduces himself. He is reviewing my medical records and asks how I know that I'm allergic to penicillin. My response is that it has been on my medical records since I was a child, and my mother is no longer alive to ask, so I don't know. We are going to experiment, he tells me. Based on the pathology reports, my body needs penicillin or some derivative of it to fight this infection. He assures me he is going to sit by my bedside with an EpiPen in hand while he hooks up a penicillin drip to my IV. Once more, my stress levels are extremely high. Hurting and exhausted, I lie there as he asks me questions to make sure no reaction is taking place. He has kind eyes, and his energy is very calm. The hour goes by, and we are good. Penicillin it is.

I'm trying to rest, which, in a hospital, is impossible. My mouth is throbbing, I can hardly open it to down liquids, my body is aching, and it feels like I can't swallow. Italian ice is my new best friend; it's, so cold and delicious going down my throat. My stomach is still upset as I wrangle with R2D2 to unplug from the wall and rush into the restroom, swearing at him occasionally. I'm constantly trying to calm myself by breathing in and out, counting, as in meditation. Four breaths in, four breaths out. I'm losing track of the days while in the hospital. Trying to gather my thoughts. The next day I am taken down for more X-rays and a CT scan.

On November 29, 2016, the doctor advises me that he will have to do another surgery. I can't have anything to eat or drink after midnight. I start crying, wanting to feel normal again without pain and discomfort.

The next day, I waited all day for an operating room to become available. Finally, at 7:00 p.m., the orderly comes to take me down for surgery. I text David immediately to let him know, but he can't come because he has the grandchildren and lives about an hour away. Luckily, Nicole is an RN on staff at the hospital was working that night. She arrives immediately and sits with me while talking with the surgeon. They wheel me in again to start another procedure.

Waking up in recovery, I am in a lot of pain while They are administering pain medication. Suddenly, blood is spurting out above me. Wait, is that mine?! The adrenaline is pumping now, waking me up. I hear them say the doctor has left but is on his way back. I watch in disbelief as they change my gown, soaked with blood. They are now applying pressure with a white towel to my neck.

I question is this it, am I on my way out. A recent memory of my brother Jim in the hospital in August flashes through my brain. We almost lost him to a bleed out. Nicole is working that night and is by my side now, telling me to look at her and squeeze her hand. She is very calm, but I am panicking, never having felt so much fear and anxiety in my whole life. I remember saying to her that I will break her fingers, and she keeps reassuring me I will not.

A familiar voice breaks through my fear. It's the doctor. A wave of relief washes over me. The last thing I remember is glancing at the clock on the wall; it was almost 10 p.m. That night, I was brought back up to my room after 11 p.m. Someone else has been moved into the room now. It is no longer quiet. I remember that all I wanted was sleep, but all I could do was stare out the hospital window at the city lights. My head and neck wrapped like a mummy, very safe and secure.

The next morning, the surgeon came in and unraveled the cloth. He said it was to be sure I didn't bleed during the night. He informed me that most of the infection was out, and the antibiotics would do the rest. The infectious disease doctor came in to advise me about the antibiotics I would be taking while at home. I wondered, will this ever end? Take deep breaths and calm yourself. I was released to go home 24 hours later. **Happy, happy, day!**

The Blue Wings of the Dragonfly

GOING HOME

"Begin each day Renewed,
Refreshed, and glad to be alive."

Norman Vincent Peale

My dear friend Judy of 34 years came to pick me up at the hospital. I arrive home on December 2, 2016, about 5:30 p.m. I'm anxious to see my dog Jazz. I had missed her so much during my two weeks stay in the hospital. Opening the door, she came running to me, wagging her tail. I wondered how she had coped being alone at night for the first time in 13 years. My friend stayed for a couple of hours, then reluctantly left me to go home to her dog. Well Jazz, it's just you and me now. She stayed by my side continually, never leaving my sight.

My whole body hurt so badly that, I ached in places I wasn't even aware I had. My mouth and lips were so swollen that I looked like someone who had a very bad Botox injection done. There were canker sores throughout my entire mouth. My face looked swollen particularly on the right side where all seven of the surgeries had taken place. I sat for a while, grateful to be home with my dog at my feet and a heating pad on my neck and jaw. Finally deciding it was dinner time for Jazz and myself, I stood up for the first time since I had been home.

What's happening? My feet, ankles, and legs were so swollen that I could hardly stand and when I did, it felt like pins and needles, very similar to your foot falling asleep after being in one position for a long time. Upon seeing myself in a full-length mirror for the first time, I notice my legs look like I've been on steroids. It was unbelievable. I make my way into the kitchen where Jazz is eagerly awaiting her dinner. I feed her then decide I will have to sip on a bowl of soup. My mouth cannot open very wide, so I use one of my son's baby spoons from years ago to feed myself. It was wonderful to be in my chair without all the hospital noises, people coming and going, thermometers, blood pressure cuffs, drawing blood and R2D2.

After the sunset and as nightfall approaches, I find myself experiencing worry and unease like something imminent is about to happen. I try to find solace in my bed with Jazz by my side but to no avail. I message a friend who is a physician's assistant. After explaining to him what I am experiencing, he says that I have PTSD (post-traumatic stress disorder) because of what I went through while in hospital. Being alone at night didn't help the situation, because 10 p.m. is the time of day I had started bleeding from a hematoma and had to be rushed back into surgery when I was in the hospital. Every night, at about that same time, I would undergo this same feeling and wait until that hour had passed. Only then could I sleep. Not in my bed but in my chair, as lying down would cause my jaw and mouth to throb.

Every morning Jazz and I would follow the same routine. I'd feed her first, then make my Cream of Wheat, which enabled me to crush the antibiotic and mix it in my bowl, so that I would be able to get it in my system. My stomach was still upset, but at least I was home and didn't have to deal with R2D2. On the fifth day home from the hospital, the swelling in my legs and feet eased to the point that I could finally see my ankle bone. I struggled every day trying to do all of my daily rituals and rest, and I walked around the house as much as I could to exercise and get some normality back in my life. Still, on liquids and soft foods, my weight was dropping steadily. The facial swelling was still there, and the drain holes under my chin were not healing normally. They were sucked in like a vacuum; the muscles in my neck were very taut and sore. My right ear hurt as well. I continued to see the surgeon and infectious disease doctors every week for five weeks.

On December 29, 2016, I have an appointment with the surgeon. X-rays are taken, and the doctor is advising me that he wants another CT scan done at the hospital. He shows me some white streaks on the X-ray picture; he doesn't think they are normal. It was not without fear that I entered that hospital to get the CT scan. Amazed at my level of anxiety, I realize this was triggering the memories of not so long ago when I had this procedure twice while in the hospital. An intravenous needle is put in, while you lie perfectly still as they inject a special dye called contrast material to help highlight the areas of your body being examined. In this case, it was my mouth. Once the dye is injected, you are informed that a warm sensation will be felt in your body, and it will feel like you have emptied your bladder, but you haven't. It is a strange sensation. During the test, you lie on a table that is attached to the scanner. The CT scanner is a large doughnut-shaped machine. It then moves you into the sphere, the picture taken, and out you come. The needle removed, this experience is over, and I, for one, am very grateful.

I see the surgeon again on January 3, 2017. He advises me that another surgery is needed, based on the CT scan. He believes the infection had gotten into the bone, and needed to be removed. He wouldn't know the extent of it until he opened me up. His office would set up a time and day based on the availability of an operating room and let me know. When I got to my car, I burst into tears, not knowing if I could get through this again on my own.

The surgery is set for January 16, 2017, at 10 a.m. I arrive two hours early to be prepped. The doctor comes in to explain everything he will be doing. It is going to be a long surgery, approximately four hours, the longest one yet. My stomach does a flip-flop. He will be making an incision under my chin and over to my right ear, about five inches in length. GULP! He'll also make one on the inside at the infection site to scrape out all the bone graft from where the titanium post had been placed. I have resigned myself to the idea now and try to stay positive, wanting this to be over. The orderly comes to take me to the operating room.

The anesthesiologist is waiting to explain his procedure and go over my reactions to medications. He advises me that unlike my prior surgeries, this time a small tube will be put up my nose to administer the anesthesia, because of the length of the surgery and he wants to stay out of the surgeon's way. Great, I think that I would rather he didn't tell me about that part. He leaves, and I am wheeled into surgery, comforted to know that when I come out my son will be there to see me. I worry about my dog being alone again at night; she has just gotten used to my being home.

The doctors have arrived. Upon opening my eyes, I am in recovery, and they are asking me about my pain level. I'm hurting, but happy the surgery is over. I have become a little loopy from the pain medication. Brought back to my room, the nurse is laughing with me as she helps me into the bed. My son arrives, and a couple of my dear friends are there as well, but I am drifting in and out of consciousness.

Everyone leaves by nightfall. I'm alone again, looking out of my hospital window at the city lights. I listen to some meditation music on YouTube and do the meditation breathing four breaths in, four breaths out calming myself. The antibiotics are wreaking havoc on my stomach again, and R2D2 and I are up off and on all night. There is a drain tube under my right ear with a plastic tube collecting blood from the incision site. It's not an attractive look at all, that and the black stitches under my neck, which resemble a corded rope. My thoughts go to Frankenstein. Morning finally arrives, bringing more blood draws and temperature and blood pressure checks.

The doctor arrives about 6 a.m. He tells me the surgery was successful and he was glad that he went back in. He did have to scrape the outside of the mandible, the largest, strongest and lowest bone in the face. It forms the lower jaw and holds the lower teeth in place. It is like an onion with lots of layers. He only had to scrape the outer layer but had to go deep in the area where the original post was put in. The doctor informs me that I can go home later today. Momentarily, I am happy.

The infectious disease doctor comes in to tell me that I will have to be kept on intravenous antibiotics for the next six weeks. A PICC line will be inserted before going home. A PICC line? My anxiety rises again. Let me get this right. It is a thin, soft, long catheter (tube) that is inserted into a vein in your arm. The tip of the catheter is positioned in a large vein that carries blood to the heart. OMG! A foreign object inserted and left in my body. I also learn that my antibiotics would be delivered to my home, and a nurse will come to teach me how to administer my intravenous antibiotics. Will this ever end? Take deep breaths and calm yourself.

I was released to go home at 5:30 p.m. that day. Finally, I'm home again with my constant companion, Jazz.

A NEW DIRECTION

"The big question is whether you are going to be able to say a hearty yes to your adventure."

Joseph Campbell

It is January 18, 2017, my first day home since the last major surgery on my jaw and mouth. Jazz is happy to see me again. My body is aching all over with flu-like symptoms. I have never had to endure such pain and suffering in my life. Taking care of myself and my regimen is a full-time job. On Sunday, January 22, 2017, a courier arrives to deliver my medication to be administered via the PICC line. He advises me to keep it refrigerated, as it has only a five-day shelf life. Upon opening the bag, I see five large syringes with antibiotic medication, other syringes with saline solution, and more syringes with heparin. Also included are alcohol wipes, bandages, and tubing.

The visiting nurses arrive the next morning to give me my first lesson. It is quite a procedure. First, they change and clean the PICC line area. The tubing is then connected. Mine had to have an extension put on since I am right-handed and couldn't administer the medicines with my left hand alone. You always cleanse the access port before attaching the infusion tubing or the medication syringe. You first flush the line with the saline and flick or tap the syringe with your finger. By doing this, it will cause any large air bubbles to rise into the tip. Slowly push on the plunger until a very tiny drop of flushing solution comes out of the tip. Then use a push-pull motion to flush the line, continue with medication administration, do another flush with saline and then a flush with heparin to prevent the clotting of blood.

I don't think I can do this, I tell her. She tells me if you can't then you'll have to drive to the profusion center every day at the same time to have a nurse perform this procedure. You can do this, says one of the nurses.

After they leave, I arrange everything on the counter in the hopes of remembering all that is needed for the next day. I have taken my notes. Oh, and by the way, when you shower do not get the bandage or area around the site wet at all, or a nurse will have to come out and change it to help prevent infection.

Sitting in my chair that night, I am reflecting on all that has happened over the last months. Hell, over the last several years. How did I get here? I put on a YouTube meditation for healing and start my breathing and relaxation. Come back to self; I think as I drift off to sleep.

Morning is here. Jazz and I do all our rituals, by 11 a.m. I need to start my new ritual, administering the solutions and antibiotics to my PICC line. I begin by taking one dose of the antibiotic out of the refrigerator allowing it to sit for about 20 minutes, so upon entering my system, it will not be so cold, one of the suggestions given by the visiting nurse. Next, I cut open the plastic coverings on the saline and heparin syringe flushes, then open the alcohol wipes. Upon first trying to tap or flick the bubbles out, I push on the syringe. The next thing I know, saline solution is everywhere, having shot up to the ceiling and across the counter. It's a good thing I have some extra of those.

After cleaning up the mess, I make another attempt. This time only a small amount escaped. The process is stressing me out. I then disconnect the saline and put the antibiotic in slowly. Five milliliters in and then I count to 60 and continue until the syringe is emptied. Because it is cooler in temperature, I feel it enter my system, giving me the strangest sensations as it traveled through my body. Another saline flush, then the heparin. By the time I clean everything up, about 45 minutes have elapsed. I'm exhausted.

Showering is even more fun. Not! The site needs to be kept dry. I try wrapping a small washcloth around the site first, then covering it with a plastic bag and putting rubber bands at both ends. Well, that didn't work very well, especially since my left hand was doing most of the work and I'm right-handed. In a couple of days, I discovered that cling wrap worked very well with a plastic bag and rubber bands at both ends. It never ceased to amaze me how tired I was. I realize now that healing, especially after trauma, takes a great deal of energy. I needed to be kinder to myself, to take care of me. It's something most of us don't think about until we are put in a situation where we have no control.

A couple of weeks go by, and the infectious disease doctor calls to say that based on pathology reports, he is changing my medication to an intravenous drip bag and adding another oral antibiotic for me to take. The new meds are delivered, and the visiting nurse comes to hook up a smaller version of R2D2, teaching me how to administer this new medicine. I now learn how to get the air bubbles out of the tubing, which, by the way, I forgot to clamp the first time and had yet again another mess to clean. My stomach is so upset from the medicines that I can hardly eat. I continue to see the doctors for the next six weeks since the last surgery.

On February 28, 2017, I see my doctor. He is concerned about an abscess and the fact that the original wound site, which I refer to as the sinkhole, is not properly closing. My anxiety is back, thinking I don't want to do another hospital stay. The doctor says they're going to take me to the clinic right now, not giving me much time to think about it, which was probably a good thing. He is going to do a procedure called a debridement, which is for the removal of any dead, devitalized or contaminated tissue; any foreign material; and any other substances that inhibit healing. He then irrigated the site and closed it with gut sutures. We discuss antibiotics, and he consults with the infectious disease doctor. They agree to stop the intravenous antibiotics and allow me to take just an oral one. I'm down 20 pounds now, and he is concerned about my weight loss.

I'm home again with ice packs and rest. The next day, the visiting nurse comes for my final blood draw and removes the PICC line. Hallelujah! A shower without bags and rubber bands. It's those little things that make for a great day. The exercises I am given to start doing at home with tongue depressors, help get my jaw open, you stack them one on top of the other and keep adding one as you slide them in the front of your mouth. Physical therapy is ordered, twice a week for however long it takes. I continued to see the surgeon once a week until June 27, 2017.

I begin physical therapy on March 30, 2017. In the first session, Lauri is very gentle, doing some stretching exercises on the outside of my face, then puts on a pair of latex gloves and, explains that she will be going inside my mouth to start stretching the mandible, or lower jawbone, and surrounding muscles. Once her fingers are inside my mouth, my teeth start chattering, and I am shaking uncontrollably. She stays there for only a few seconds, removing her hand from my face. I am still shaking, and she puts a warm compress around my neck and face. I start to calm down, and the shaking stops. She explains to me that what I experienced was a trauma release. Muscles have memory, and when she went inside my mouth, the muscles registered pain. They were trying to protect me from being hurt again. It's amazing how the human body works.

Lauri also gave me exercises to do while sitting in my chair at home, including putting my own hands in my mouth to stretch and desensitize the area. I decided to create a couple of phrases that would help me while I was being worked on in physical therapy. As I lay on the table during my next session, when she puts her hand inside my mouth, I keep repeating silently to myself. "At this moment, I have always been safe," and "I surrender to the healing." It worked. My mouth and jaw are tired and sore. It has been twelve months now, and the therapy continues. The osteopath also works on aligning the meridians and areas that have become blocked because of the trauma my body has undergone. A naturopathic doctor works with me in getting the nutrients that my body needs. I get IV drips of vitamins, B and C and minerals to replenish and speed my recovery from all the months of antibiotics and anesthesia during the surgeries. Loss, even that of a tooth, is grieved by the body. It was a part of me that cannot be replaced.

SNOWFLAKES, A DREAM

"In the garden of memory, in the palace of dreams ... that is where you and I shall meet."

Alice Through the Looking Glass

I am old, sitting by a window in my favorite chair contemplating my life and all the things I have been through, all I have done. Snow is falling outside very gently collecting on the ground. The sun is coming up slowly through the trees. I sip my warm tea from one of my favorite china cups, pale cream with tiny roses around the edges. I smile, remembering winters of long ago. The snow sparkles as the sun's rays touch it like glistening diamonds. It's very peaceful.

Then I think about snowflakes, beautiful feathery ice crystals. How they are all different, not one alike. Was that the divine source's plan? For what purpose? Perhaps it was so that we can learn from each other to embrace our differences. Our time here is very short. Why did I take so long to realize that?

How am I feeling? Accomplished and, tired but happy inside. My life has been interesting so far. It is complex, happy, and sad. At times overwhelming. My journey has taken me on many paths that have crossed with so many other people all going through their lessons. I'm grateful for all the people that have come into this life. Some I knew from before, others are brand-new. I can sense their energies. Some have moved on, while others still here are caught in moments of time. What is time? It doesn't exist anywhere else. I have been there and seen. Time is another coping mechanism for this existence. What now needs to be completed?

As I savor the warm tea "Earl Grey," my favorite, the aroma fills my senses. The bergamot citrus permeates the air, almost like perfume. I shall certainly miss this one day when I have moved on. So many wonderful things in my life. Some were tragic, but some were extraordinary they brought me to my soul's depth to learn who I Am. Where my strengths lie, and where my weaknesses are. I understand these now but not before this. I had only caught glimpses of them. Now, with the serenity of the snow falling and, the fire crackling in the fireplace, these things all have memories for me. Why do we hold on to our memories? Do they help us cope with our responsibilities and problems calmly and adequately? To reflect, to remember, over time only the good memories remain. Is the mind built that way, so we can survive, endure, push through the pain, and come out on the other side? I have been lucky in many ways. I'm realizing now that gratitude is immense. We need to appreciate every moment and give gratitude for the moments we have.

C. Lee Roggeman

FATHER

How does a father show a child the way when he is lost? A father is supposed to be your protector, to help guide you, to love you. With my father, this was not the case. He was brilliant, creative, driven, and emotional, with a great sense of humor. He also had another side to him, like Dr. Jekyll and Mr. Hyde, which usually came out when he would drink. Yes, my father was an alcoholic, albeit a very high-functioning one. He was also bipolar and manic. Because of his insecurities, he was a tyrant who instilled fear; he was very manipulative, even cruel at times.

Financially, he was a good provider. He was always busy wearing many hats: an architect, a builder, a teacher, a natural musician. He could make that saxophone sing in his jazz band. He built every home that we resided. His designs were innovative and way ahead of their time. We had a toaster built into the wall and a central vacuuming system. For a home built in the sixties that was pretty remarkable. My dad owned a lot of land on one particular street in our city. We would keep moving down the street into every new home he would build. I remember pulling my red wagon down the street to bring him ice cold Coca-Cola to drink while watching him pound nails first with his right hand, then with his left. He was ambidextrous.

However, my father had sadness that remained just beneath the surface. Ours was a love-hate relationship. How do you love someone who is never there for you emotionally? I was the oldest of four, which made me the guinea pig. Rules were made for me that, by the time my sister and brothers were in high school, had somehow changed. Perhaps he had mellowed, softened a bit. Not in time for me, though.

After graduating high school and going through a failed relationship, I left New York and moved to Arizona. I wanted to get as far away from my father's energy as I could. I can still see my mother's face from the kitchen window, tears in her eyes as I drove away. He would still call on occasion but usually when he was drunk, and I would tell him not to call when he had been drinking. The calls became fewer and fewer as time went on. Did I miss him? It's hard to say.

DEATH BY SLOW SUICIDE

"People fear death even more than pain. It's strange that they fear death. Life hurts a lot more than death. At the point of death, the pain is over. Yeah, I guess it is a friend."

Jim Morrison

It was September 1987. I received a phone call from my brother saying he didn't know how long my father had to live. I started checking flights and made my reservations for the first week of October, which would include my birthday. I had left New York after the blizzard of 1978 and never looked back. Through the years, I watched as my father would drink and smoke, lighting one cigarette after another and chasing it down with alcohol.

In earlier years, there were periods of time where he wouldn't drink at all. Those were the good times. However, it was like walking on eggshells; you never knew which dad would be coming through the door that day or night. Alcohol made what would seem like a funny and loving father into one I did not recognize. One day, when I was old enough, I asked him why he drank. His answer was, "If I don't drink, I feel like I'm standing in the middle of a railroad track with a train headed straight for me, and I can't move in either direction." He said the alcohol took that feeling away. In other words, it numbed that feeling. I tried to grasp this, but it was out of my reach.

Memories flood back to me. Memories of the nights he would be drinking and yelling, hitting my mother. I would gather my sister and brothers like a mother hen, putting them in one of the bedroom closets with pillows and blankets to keep them safe. I'd gather clothes for the next few days and put them in a paper bag. Once things were quiet and he had passed out, my mom would come in to get us. We would quietly sneak out and pile into the car, and she would drive us to our Nonni's or my Aunt Mae's house, where we would stay until he would sober up. He'd come by a few days later with candy and fruit for us kids and sweet talk my mom into coming back home again.

The pilot announces our arrival into Buffalo. As the wheels of the plane hit the tarmac, I'm startled back to reality. Gazing out the window at the grey skies, I feel depressed. It's been ten years since I had returned to my hometown. Time for my happy face. I stay with my Aunt Lou, my dad's sister and by nightfall, my system is getting the worst head cold. Is it stress, anxiety, or the fact that I am freezing? The temperatures were unusually cold that year.

The following morning, I stepped through the sliding glass doors of the hospital and walked slowly down the hallway to his room. My youngest brother was already there. My eyes were glued to the bed. I was shocked by how old my father looked. His eyes were bulging, his skin was a sick yellow color, as were the whites of his eyes. His stomach was distended, and it looked like he was nine months pregnant. He smiled when our eyes met. His teeth had been pulled out years before because his gums were in such bad shape from the disease. My son, who had only seen him a couple of times, referred to him as "Grandpa No Teeth."

My emotions ran the whole gamut from sadness and anger too, empathy and love. I pulled up a chair next to his hospital bed. He said he was glad I came. He wanted to apologize for everything he had done, not realizing at the time the suffering and grief he had caused, especially to me. I forgave him, but I knew in my heart that if he had the chance to do it all over again, nothing would change. His favorite song was "I Did It My Way" by Frank Sinatra.

Looking down at him as he drifted off to sleep, I remember a time at my uncle's house with all the cousins gathered around. He was drunk again, but this time he had one of my uncle's guns in his hand, threatening to shoot himself. Panic filled the air until my Uncle John managed to get the gun out of his hands, and he started crying. On the drive home, we would all sing songs. It helped relieve the tension until we pulled into our driveway. We were home, not sure how safe and sound.

At the hospital, I sat in silence, just holding his hand. My sister Trisha arrived, which provided some relief. For whatever ever reason, she was always more connected to him than I was. Perhaps because I was the oldest, I was witness to a lot more of what was going on over the years.

It was a very long week. When I left the hospital to go home, I leaned over and kissed my dad on the forehead, telling him that I loved and forgave him. It was the last time I would see my father alive.

On the night he died, I woke up about 3:30 a.m. MST and started crying. I knew he was gone. My brother called to say my dad had passed away about 6:30 a.m. Eastern time. He died on November 2, 1987. I didn't return home for his services. I was a single mom at the time and couldn't afford to go back. I was grateful I had the opportunity to see him while he was still living. He was the first parent I would lose, but not the first death I would experience.

MEMORY OVERLOAD

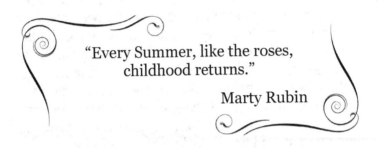

"Every Summer, like the roses, childhood returns."

Marty Rubin

The sun is shining brightly; the skies are blue. I walk outside to lie down in the hammock. A slight breeze blows across my face bringing with it the delicious fresh scent of cut grass. I have always loved that smell and the sweet whiff of a watermelon just after you cut it open, the taste of a crisp apple in the fall, peaches sweet and ripe with juice running down your chin, and ripe red tomatoes on the vine in the garden. I would often sneak a salt shaker out with me to sprinkle on the tomato before biting into it.

Suntan lotion, riding horses and the smell of leather from the saddle which I always found quite sensual. A field of fresh cut hay in the distance, freshly turned soil, and burgers sizzling on the grill. All of these things I remember from childhood. Good memories.

Every year around the Fourth of July, Mom and Dad would take us to pick sweet cherries at Farmer John's Orchards. We would climb the trees and reach for the furthest ones out, usually because they were the ripest. We'd eat as many as we picked. Our parents always knew when we were done because then the cherry fights would start, throwing them at each other laughing. So homeward-bound we would be, with bags of fresh cherries. Strawberries were next, warmed by the sun, and the jam to be made and stored for the cold winter to follow.

Fall was my favorite time of year. The leaves turned wondrous colors of orange, red, and yellow. My siblings and I would rake and pile them into a large heap on the ground and then run and jump into the leaves, scattering them everywhere. I remember one fall day my younger brother Jim jumped into the leaves, only to discover he had landed in a pile of dog poop. We all laughed so hard our sides hurt and tears streamed down our faces.

We forget about these happy times as we grow older and get caught up in the mainstream of life. Responsibilities, school, work, family. Somewhere, we lose a part of ourselves. It's important to remember what brings us joy and makes us smile; we need to take time every day to reflect back on the good times, appreciating times when life was less complicated. There is a strong need to connect with the moments that bring comfort and a sense of peace in our life.

There were times I would lie on the grass in our yard, looking up and observing the different shapes in the clouds. There are animal faces and birds, all there for moments; as the sky changes, so do they. The clouds undergo a gradual process of transformation. We change as well. Life brings us challenges that we can't ignore, some life-altering. We must persist, embrace, surrender and trust.

I take in the sweet fragrance of clover, searching for that four-leaf one. I watch the honeybees flutter over them, gathering nectar. Einstein said that one day the bee's survival would be in danger and they are. How did this happen, and what does it mean for our future? How did Einstein know what he did; higher consciousness? The same thing we are capable of if we quiet our mind and set our ego aside. We must take the time to connect with source energy and go within. Only there will we find our true answers.

It feels good to remember things that bring us joy. Newly fallen snow and the milkman delivering milk in glass bottles to our door, partially frozen. Mom would let us add a little sugar, calling it snow ice cream. We thought it was the greatest. Waking up to the radio announcing there would be no school that day because of all the snow that had fallen during the night. It was eerie and peaceful at the same time. Mom would bundle us up so much that we could hardly walk as we headed outside to make snow angels and snowmen and have the inevitable snowball fights. Tobogganing down the hillside, with a mixture of fear and laughter, until we would crash or fall off. Looking up to see the sun hitting the icicles hanging from the roof, as they start slowly melting and dripping, glistening in the light.

My dog, Lady, was a beautiful collie who was always by my side everywhere I went. I remember getting her on my eighth birthday. It was a surprise. My dad and mom said we were going for a ride. We all piled into the car, driving through the winding country roads until we arrived at a farm with a huge red barn. We all got out of the car, and Dad greeted the man coming out of his home. As we headed to the barn, I wondered what was in there.

Sure enough, there were nine puppies, so happy and playful. Dad said, "Happy Birthday! Pick one, and it's yours." I was so excited I could hardly stand it! The smell of puppies is unlike any other. Smiling, I picked this fat, fluffy little female. She seemed shy but approached me. She was the one. Lady and I were best buddies for years to come. Why do we have to grow up? Now, I wish I could go back. Wait... I just did. Memories are important. They create a part of who we are and who we become.

MOTHER

How does a daughter grow up without a mother? My mother was very loving and caring, gentle and kind. How she managed this, I will never know. When she was three years old, her mother died. She grew up in Huntsville, Alabama, in a poor family. My grandfather, her father whom we referred to as "Big Daddy," worked on a cotton farm with ten children to raise. My mom was ninth in the birth order.

A mother represents comfort and security, no matter our age. We lose a part of our identity without her. She had a stepmother who rejected her. Some of her siblings were already grown and out of the house by the time her mother died. I believe she perceived herself, at times, as helpless and powerless against adversity.

The loss of a mother is a part of life, just like a heartbeat, the sun rising and nightfall. At the age of 16, my mother left home and came to New York, where one of her older sisters my Aunt Mae owned a restaurant. She decided to finish her senior year of high school there while working at the restaurant part-time. She met and married my father at the age of 17, looking for some stability in her life. Little did she know the life she would choose to take on.

She was quiet, stoic, supportive, intelligent, creative, and funny. I remember her laugh, her smile. My best friend, my confidant, and my only constant while growing up.

She moved to Arizona shortly after David was born, and was a great help to me. We remained close until the day she died.

I believe that from the loss of a mother we learn to take responsibility for ourselves, and hopefully move into a place where we can care for ourselves both emotionally and physically. She was a survivor; beneath that subtle exterior was a strength with resilience and determination. The strength she somehow would pass on to me. It is with much gratitude and love that I am thankful for the mother to whom I was born.

DEATH RATTLE

I remember the day as if it were yesterday. I was sitting at my desk working on a tile design when the phone call came from my husband Darryl, saying that my mom had called, telling him she couldn't breathe. He was already on his way to her house and had called 911. I felt as if the wind had been knocked out of my sails. I hung up the phone, grabbed my keys and was in my car within minutes, heading down the freeway to meet them at the ER.

I immediately started calling my sister and two brothers who lived out of state to let them know, so they could start making flight arrangements. Every red light seemed like an eternity. My heart beat faster and faster. Why wasn't the light changing already? Darryl said she was talking as they loaded her into the ambulance and her oxygen rate was at 94. Then, a song came on the radio: "I Hope You Dance" by Lee Ann Womack. At that moment, I could feel her presence wash over me like a wave in the ocean. I sensed something had gone wrong.

Entering the emergency room, I ran to the front desk to ask about my mother. A woman came up to my husband and me, and she escorted us back to an office. I just wanted to see my mother! She proceeded to say that while the ambulance was en route to the hospital, my mother had suffered a major heart attack. She was in a coma, being kept alive by machines. It was a very grave situation, and it hit me hard as if someone had punched me in the gut. Warm tears started streaming down my face, it felt like salt being rubbed in an open wound. How could this happen? I stared at Darryl in disbelief, angry that he had let this happen to her. We were led to a room where my mother lay hooked up to machines, tubes coming out of her nose and mouth. Her eyes were open like small slits, but there was no movement. I held her hand, begging her to come back. Don't leave like this! There are so many things I need to say, to tell you how much I love you. Time stood still, for how long I don't know.

A doctor came in to say that he could move her to ICU, but he had no hope. The machine was pumping what was left of her heart, and there was no brain activity. Or I could let her go unplugging all the systems. I knew she would no longer want to be kept alive like this. I watched him disconnect the machines while I stroked her beautiful hair. He walked out of the room for a moment, and as I sat with her, I held her hand and I heard the final gasp of air out of her lungs. It was a gurgling, crackling sound like blowing air through a straw at the bottom of a cup of water. The death rattle, they call it.

I sat there in disbelief. The doctor announced the date and time of death on August 21, 2001. She was only 65 years old. I watched as they covered her face and wheeled her out of the room. That's the last I would see of her physical body. Walking out of the hospital as the sun hit my face, I could feel the intense heat of the day; I dropped to my knees, and a loud guttural sound came from my body, like that of a wounded animal.

LIFE AND DEATH LESSONS

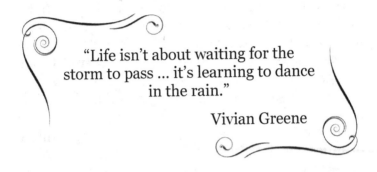

"Life isn't about waiting for the storm to pass ... it's learning to dance in the rain."

Vivian Greene

Death comes in so many forms. It could be the ending of an idea, the ending of a job, a failed relationship, the loss of a loved one, someone we knew from childhood, or a beloved pet. Suffering is a part of humanity, a form of contentment and healing. It's about self-actualization. Our thoughts are vibrations, and energy works like a boomerang. Be aware of your thoughts. What you put out there comes back to you. To me this begs the question; are we predisposed to the events that take place in our lives? I believe it is how we handle what comes our way that matters. No one has a perfect childhood, a perfect marriage, or a perfect life. How do we cope with what life brings us? That comes from a place within. Some people never find their way; others seem to breeze through life.

We are all here on our own soul's journey. None of us experience life the same. Our parents weren't born knowing how to raise us. Hell, their parents didn't know much more. We must find ourselves and dig deep to discover our core beliefs. Follow your passion, discover your gifts, allow intuition to guide you, and surrender to the process. Life passes quickly. You must reach out and grab it, or you will lose it. We must grow our wings and soar, embody our potential. By doing this, life will be simple and less complicated.

Life can be whatever you want it to be. Full of promise, aspirations, and hope. These are such uncertain times in which we live. There is a light at the end of the tunnel, but you need to believe that, and you have to feel it in your heart. You were not meant to sit on the sidelines, but, instead, to throw yourself into life, taking risks and doing something out of your comfort zone. Enjoy the ride! And how do you do this? By letting go. You think you have control, but you don't. It's just an illusion you have created for yourself.

It is time to get back to the pure and uncomplicated things in life. It's time to reconnect with self and, know who you are. Accept and love yourself, for you are perfect in and of yourself. Find someone to share that love, those moments in time. Look in the mirror and realize your potential; nothing can stop you. We are all here to experience things, to use our five senses. What a wonderful gift that is! When all five of our senses are involved, life is amazing. At the end of your life, what do you want? Regret, sadness and pain because of circumstances or choices, made in the past. Hours of hopelessness or a life filled with joy, and passion and love, the essence of our being. The feel-good things, I call them.

C. Lee Roggeman

THE SINGLE WHITE ROSE

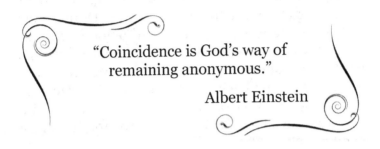

"Coincidence is God's way of
remaining anonymous."

Albert Einstein

The year is 1985. My son is almost five years old. I
have been dating since the divorce with a lot of
frustration and not much luck. I'm journaling
every night and asking for guidance. One night I
decided to completely turn it over to a divine
source, leaving it in the hands of the powers that
be to bring me the next love of my life. A good
man. Thinking about it, I would need a sign. I
asked to receive a single white rose from the
person chosen for me.

About six months later I met Darryl. We were
both building a home in the same subdivision. He
asked for some design help with his new home. I
agreed, and the work began, choosing furniture,
mirrors, window treatments, and paint colors.
Several times he would ask me to join him for
dinner, but I was reluctant. Mixing business with
pleasure usually didn't end well. Honestly, I wasn't

that interested. Three months later he came by to give me his final payment for the design work. When the work was complete, he asked about dinner again. I finally agreed to go. Dinner was very nice. He was intelligent, had a good sense of humor, was good-looking, and seemed to love his work as an aerospace engineer. He was also very good with David. Golf was his passion. He was almost 15 years older than I which seemed a little scary at the time. I decided he probably wasn't a good match for me.

Five days later, my mom and I were unpacking boxes, and the doorbell rang. Upon opening the door, there stood a young man from a florist shop, and he handed me a bouquet of roses. One dozen red and a single white rose in the center with a card attached. Immediately, I felt a wave of nausea. I ran to the restroom and began to throw up. Hearing all the commotion, mom came to check on me. She then saw the roses, sitting on the dining room table, knowing about my pact with the divine source. Smiling, she said, "There is a single white rose." Upset, I reach over for the attached card. It read: To Cindy, someone very special in my life. P.S. You ask why the single white rose? D.R. (his Nickname) **Seriously, Universe?**

I didn't feel well. I didn't think that Darryl was the one. Be careful what you ask for you; might just get it! Later that day he called to ask if I had received the flowers. I told him yes and thanked him. He asked if I wanted to go to dinner that night. Was I ready to stare my destiny in the face? I agreed. While we were having dinner, I inquired about the single white rose. He replied that while he was driving to work that day, he saw the florist shop and pulled over. Upon going inside, he said he wanted to show me somehow that I was different from all the rest. He said, "You were the white rose amongst the red."

For the next 22 years, until his death, I received one dozen red roses with a single white rose in the center for every anniversary. I did not tell him about the entry in my journal to the source, until two years later when we were married.

C. Lee Roggeman

A LONG JOURNEY TO DEATH

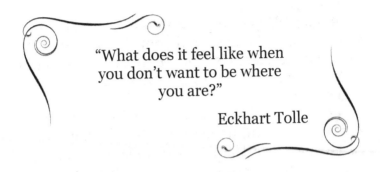

"What does it feel like when
you don't want to be where
you are?"

Eckhart Tolle

It was July of 1986. I woke up in the middle of the night. I sat up in bed; the room was freezing. I glanced at the clock. It was 3:10 a.m. Where was Darryl? Walking out to the living room, I saw him sitting on the sofa; a pillow clutched to his chest. All the windows were wide open, which explained why it was so cold.

"What's wrong," I ask.

"I can't breathe," he keeps saying.

I immediately ask if he has any pain in his arm or jaw, to which he replies, "Yes!" Knowing something needs to be done, I reach for the phone to dial 911, but he stops me, saying he doesn't want to go in an ambulance.

"Then get your ass in my car," I say. "We're going to the emergency room!"

My hands are shaking as I'm driving. Anxious, adrenaline pumping, going through red lights when I could. Darryl looks over at me and asks me to pull over. Are you kidding right now! He's going to be sick.

Reluctantly, I stop by the side of the road. Darryl opens the door and vomits. Driving again thinking, he is having a heart attack, and we both know it. I silently say to myself, "Please don't let him die on me."

Pulling up to the emergency room doors, I frantically run in, telling them that he appears to be having a heart attack. He walks in, and a girl sitting behind the desk asks for his insurance card. He throws his wallet at her, startling both of us. A nurse takes him back immediately, and they start hooking him up to machines and drawing blood. He looks pale, and even his blue eyes are grey.

As the pain medicine starts to kick in, he begins breathing easier. After what seems like an eternity, the doctor comes in and introduces himself. As luck would have it, he is head of cardiology and happens to be on staff that night. He tells us that Darryl has suffered a major heart attack and will have to be taken into surgery to do an angioplasty, a procedure where a catheter with a small balloon tip is guided through the narrowing in your artery. Once in place, the balloon is inflated to push the plaque and stretch the artery open to boost blood flow to the heart. It is normally about an hour-long procedure. Prepped and ready, Darryl is wheeled off down the long corridor.

I am waiting patiently in a room to hear how he is doing. Two hours go by, then three. It's agonizing. I call his oldest son Jack around 7:00 a.m. to let him know what is happening and ask him to advise his three siblings as to what is going on. After five hours, the doctor enters the room to let me know that during the angioplasty procedure, one of Darryl's veins tore and they had to move fast and take him in for open heart surgery, where they did a quadruple bypass. He is resting easy, and I would be able to see him soon.

As I entered his room in the intensive care unit, he looked peaceful to me. He was hooked up to intravenous bags with tubes everywhere, but I felt somewhat relieved, knowing his pain was eased. There's one hell of a scar down his chest and his leg as well.

I sit there quietly, just observing his breathing. Slowly, his eyes opened. He half smiled when he saw me. I explained to him exactly what had happened, and he just listened. The drugs were keeping him calm and out of pain. Later we would laugh, but right now none of it was funny.

He was up and walking within 24 hours to keep pneumonia from setting in. He wanted Campbell's chicken noodle soup with saltine crackers his comfort food ever since he was a kid. I would bring it in a thermos for him every day. He would call me his angel. On day six, he was released to go home. We would see the cardiologist in a week.

His spirits seem lifted. He was happy to be alive, something most of us don't think about daily.

His cardiologist was remarkable. On our first visit, he told us that Darryl's heart had suffered a major attack, he had about 52 percent function left, and his lungs were in bad shape from all the years of smoking. Cardiac rehabilitation for six weeks was first on the list, and then he could go back to work, providing he was strong enough and with his doctor's approval. He was determined to return to work and get back in the game again: to breathe, wake up, open his eyes, and feel good both mentally and physically.

THE SAGA CONTINUES

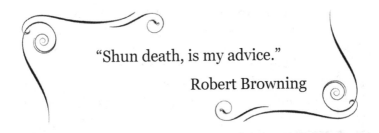

"Shun death, is my advice."

Robert Browning

Over the next nine years, he would have several smaller heart attacks and seven stents put in. A stent is a tiny tube that the doctor can insert into a blocked artery or passageway to keep it open. Darryl even had one stent re-radiated to open it again, as it had become blocked over the years. The cardiologist allowed me to come in and watch while he was performing one. I put on the blue shoe covers and a gown with a mask and gloves.

I entered the room, which seemed like a huge tent draped on all sides. It was extremely cold. A huge screen, like television, was behind the table. My husband was lying on the metal table, groggy but not fully out. They needed him to be awake enough to tell them if he feels any pain while they are performing the procedure.

I was mesmerized by all the veins and arteries, the heart pumping on the screen. I watched as they carefully threaded this minute tube up through the groin area with such precision, diligently placing the stent and then pulling the tube out. I remember bloody latex gloves on the floor and the white sheet with blood splattering on it. It went by so quickly. The human body is amazing, complicated and intricate. The frailty of it is unbelievable. It's a fascinating machine. I exited and removed my hospital gown and shoe coverings to head back up to the hospital room where he would be brought back to in the ICU. (intensive care unit) He had to lie completely flat on his back for 24 hours with an ice pack over the area to prevent bleeding. After that, we prepared to go home. He is a trooper. I don't remember him complaining, just continuing to proceed with whatever needed to be done.

So many hours and days were spent in hospital rooms and doctor's offices over the years. I lost track after a while. Even though he was going through all of this, he remained defiant in many ways. Not following his diet and, continuing to smoke, almost like he was saying, "Screw you, Universe. I'm going to do what I want, and you can't stop me."

One day, he said, "I believe that when your page is up in the book, it's up no matter what you do." What book?! I would have preferred a more quality of life attitude, even though it was his journey. All I could do was to be loving, supportive and present, even though this seemed like Pandora's Box was about to be opened.

A NEW REALITY

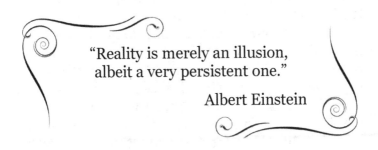

"Reality is merely an illusion,
albeit a very persistent one."

Albert Einstein

It was early in the evening on April 4, 1994. Darryl started having chest pains. He was admitted to the emergency room and then put in the hospital. He had suffered another heart attack. When he was resting peacefully later that evening, the doctor told me to go home and get some rest.

I was sound asleep when the phone rang at 4:30 a.m., it startled me. For a moment I didn't know where I was. It was the hospital calling to tell me that Darryl was having several heart attacks in a row and that I should get there immediately. I quickly dressed and headed over. By the time I arrived, he was resting peacefully again. A new doctor entered the room, and he advised me that his heart was very damaged, and because of the smoking, his lungs were severely compromised. He said another surgery wouldn't help, that he would die on the table. I was so upset with this doctor. How did he become judge and executioner? You never take away someone's hope! I told him, "You are an asshole." That was the last we would see of him.

The next morning, we went home. I contacted my friend Maree who worked for a world-renowned heart surgeon who specialized in preemie babies. I wanted a second opinion. He agreed to talk with Darryl's cardiologist and view the films. Two days later, he asked if we could come to his office for a consultation. We walked into his office. He was young, about 38 years of age, with a nice smile and a calm demeanor. He told us that after reviewing everything, he felt it was possible to have a successful surgery. It would be long and involved, but he was confident. Ultimately, he left the decision to us. Darryl looked at me and said, "Let's do this."

Three days later, he went into open heart surgery for the second time. I sat in the waiting room surrounded by family and friends. The perfusionist, a specialized healthcare professional who uses the heart-lung machine during cardiac surgeries that require a cardiopulmonary bypass to manage the patient's physiological status, kept coming out to let me know that he was doing OK, holding his own. The surgery took eight hours. The surgeon came out and advised me that he had done a quintuple by-pass, but Darryl had done just fine. He told me that I could go to his intensive care room and that they would be bringing him up shortly. I thanked the doctor and breathed a big sigh of relief. We had made the right choice.

I headed up to the room waiting for his return, and a short time later, they wheeled him in. Unfortunately for me, they had not cleaned him up after the surgery. I have never seen so much blood on any human body before let alone my husbands. His entire chest was covered in blood, as were the sheets and tubes coming from all directions. My knees started to feel like jelly. One of the nurses caught me out of the corner of her eye, and quickly grabbed a chair, told me to sit down with my head between my legs, and breathe. I did.

Slowly regaining my composure, I left the room and walked down the hall. My whole body started shaking, my teeth chattered, and tears streamed down my cheeks. I went to the restroom and splashed my face with water. Upon returning to the room, I sat in a chair. He was resting peacefully. Somehow, the certainty of my immortality was, I don't know, diminished. The cardiologist came in after a while, took one look at me, and told me I needed to go home, and rest and that Darryl would be sleeping for a while.

I got home, and exhaustion hit me. Feeling like a rag doll, I laid my head down on the bed and fell fast asleep.

The next day, I brought Darryl his all-time favorite: chicken noodle soup. He was constantly saying, "I can't breathe, something isn't right." I advised the nurses, and they said as soon as the surgeon came in they would let him know. Later that day, the doctor came in and listened to Darryl's lungs. The next thing I knew, he was barking orders at the nurses. Instruments and a chest tube were brought in. The doctor was moving fast.

Looking directly at Darryl, he said, "You're not going to like me very much." The next thing I saw was a small instrument with a blade. He quickly made a cut, and then with a hard hit to the chest using his hand, he inserted a small-bore catheter chest tube into the pleural space to remove air. The collapsed lung should re-inflate as the pressure on the lung decreases. When Darryl looked at me, still astounded by what had just happened, he joked and said, "Are we having fun yet?" I laughed out loud for the first time in a long time, as did he, while wincing with pain. I couldn't help but think: This hospital chair was not my favorite place to be anymore.

Darryl would come home a few days later. This time, though, he would be on oxygen. Tanks are delivered, and an oxygen concentrator had to be used at night while he was sleeping. It was an adjustment. The concentrator made a whirring sound, and every time he would crimp the plastic tubing line, an annoying beeping sound would go off until I nudged him to move and it would straighten out again.

He seemed to sleep fine. In six weeks, it was time for our visit with the cardiologist. We were hopeful until Darryl asked when he could go back to work. The doctor told him that his heart and lung function was low with a lot of sustained damage. He put Darryl on medical disability. The news was a tremendous blow to Darryl. He loved his work and had come up the ranks from being a machinist all the way to corporate as the international liaison for the jet engine division for Honeywell. It was the first time I ever saw him break down and cry. We drove home in silence. I wondered. What would he do now? We would be together 24/7. How is that going to work?

The first thing we did in the weeks to follow was buying a computer. I thought Darryl might enjoy that. He learned quite a bit about it but soon became bored. So, he could continue to golf; we purchased a small oxygen tank he could conceal in a backpack. No longer able to walk the course, he obtained a handicap sticker, and the golf cart could be driven right to where they were playing. It was a good thing!

I started making a line of pottery, having to re-invent myself as well. We would drive up to Prescott and Sedona to make deliveries and find new places to eat and visit. Bonsai trees became his next passion. He'd sit for hours tediously trimming and shaping them, but he soon tired of that as well. Then one day at a ceramic store I spotted a ceramic Christmas tree, and I remembered my dad and family making these when I was a child. We now had a new hobby. I would do the cleaning and glazing and firing of the trees. He would put his engineering skills to use, drilling the holes with precision to wire a set of electrical tree lights in them. We made one for each family member and some friends. We also sold a few. They were quite stunning.

Mosaics became the next passion: rolling clay, cutting out pieces, painting and firing them. He even created a wooden board for me, which enabled me to roll out the clay evenly. We also enjoyed going to my son's high school football games. Those were exciting times. Life was now very different.

When you become the caregiver, which is something I have done a great deal of in my life, you tend to lose your own identity. I kept trying to remake mine, as did he.

SPIRIT IN THE SKY

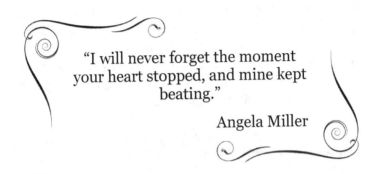

"I will never forget the moment
your heart stopped, and mine kept
beating."

Angela Miller

The last year of Darryl's life, he could no longer play golf. He was tired, and after another visit to the cardiologist, a decision was made to put a pacemaker/defibrillator in to help his heart, as it was becoming weaker. He went back into the hospital, and the procedure was completed. For the most part, he always seemed to be in good spirits. I must say, he never lost his appetite. He loved to eat. It was the one enjoyment he said they couldn't take away from him.

On June 9, 2005, at 3:30 a.m. I awoke, as I often did when Darryl got out of bed. I listened carefully. As I was getting up out of bed, I saw that he was leaning over one of the bathroom sinks. I asked him if he needed help? He kept saying I can't breathe. I told him to hold on to me as I started guiding him back to the bed so that I could get his oxygen back on him. All at once, he collapsed to the floor, jarring my vanity on the way down. Things were flying in all directions as a lamp came crashing to the floor. My heart was racing, adrenaline pumping. He was a big guy, about six feet tall, 240 pounds. I quickly dialed 911, and they stayed on the phone with me. I rolled him onto his back, trying to perform CPR. Suddenly my mouth had this unmistakable, haunting metallic taste. His eyes rolled back. What is happening? He wasn't responding.

Tears welled up in my eyes. I quickly ran to unlock the front door before the paramedics arrived. I ran back to the bedroom. He was not responsive and was ashen in color. I knew he was gone. The paramedics started to use paddles to shock him electrically. I told them he had a DNR (do not resuscitate) on file. They made a quick phone call to confirm and ceased what they were doing. He was pronounced dead at 3:45 a.m. The paramedic told me his heart had burst and his lungs had filled with blood. The only thing still pumping was the pacemaker/defibrillator in his chest. It was surreal to see him lying there on the bedroom floor.

The paramedic asked if I was alright. I looked at him, confused. "You have blood on your face." He said.

"Oh, I tried to give him CPR," I said. "That was his blood on my face."

I walked to the sink and washed it off. I dialed my son's phone number. He lived about 10 minutes away, and when he arrived, the paramedics, six of them, were standing military fashion in the entryway. Upon seeing this, my son looked at me and dropped to his knees on the floor. He wanted to go back to the bedroom; I stopped him.

"You don't want that to be your last memory," I said. "It should be a happy one." Agreeing, he came and sat with me in the living room. They were waiting for a call from the mortuary office. Procedure. The call came in, and we watched as his body, draped with a white cloth, was carried out on a stretcher.

His long-fought battle was finally over. I felt numb. My son left to go to his classes at college that day. Going back to the bedroom, I was left to clean up death's fecal discharge, the broken glass on the floor, and everything else that had flown off the vanity that night. I started to make all the necessary calls to his children and prepared for the days to come. Crawling into bed that night, I realized how quiet the house had become without the swooshing noise of the concentrator and the beeping of the oxygen tube being closed off. I don't remember sleeping much that night.

The reason this chapter is called Spirit in The Sky is that was Darryl's favorite song. When it would come on the radio in his red Corvette, he would turn it up as loud as he could, glancing over at me saying, "I want this song played at my memorial service." And it was. To this day when I hear it play on the radio, I smile.

UNEXPECTED JOURNEY

"We can only be said to be alive in those moments when our hearts are conscious of our treasures."

Thornton Wilder

The year is 2008, just three years after my husband has passed. I'm headed out the door to meet a friend. We are going to an art festival, one of my favorite things to do. As we start to walk in, my right toe gets caught in a rupture in the sidewalk. It throws me forward fast. The next thing I know, my knees hit the concrete, and I brace myself with the palm of my hands, flinging my head backward to prevent it from hitting the pavement. My phone goes flying out of my hand; things scatter out of my purse as it hits the ground. What just happened?

People are helping me up off the sidewalk asking if I'm OK. My friend asks if I need to go to the hospital. Slowly assessing the situation, I move my fingers and neck. My knees seem to be a bit scraped and bruised, but all seems to be well. "Let's go into the show," I say.

It is a beautiful sunny day with not a cloud in the sky. I feel the warmth of the sun on my face. We walk around admiring the artist's work. There are oil paintings, watercolors, blown glass, ceramic bowls, and mugs. Coming upon a booth with hand-made silver jewelry, I walk over to look inside the glass. Amongst the pieces, there is a ring and earrings with a lustrous pearl that is flat with a simple silver design around it. I make my purchase, and we continue to walk around while admiring my new ring and earrings.

As we walk, the smells of the wonderful food vendors drift through the air. Indian fry bread with powdered sugar is the first thing on the menu. Walking farther, I opt for a yummy gyro sandwich with curly fries, chocolate-covered strawberries on a stick, and, of course, a bag of warm kettle corn to take with me.

Returning home, all is well, or so I thought. A month goes by, and I'm sitting at home starting to unscrew the top of a plastic water bottle. A sharp pain shoots up my right arm, almost causing me to drop the bottle. I make a doctor's appointment. Upon examining my wrist, he sends me for an X-ray, which reveals that I have two fractures in my wrist.

A cast is put on and, the doctor says it will heal in about three weeks. It is the first time I've broken a bone in my life. When I go to work the next day, my boss questions me, and I explain that the cast will be on for three weeks. My work involved bringing tiles and floor samples out to designers and architects. He tells that I probably cannot perform these functions. We agree that I will take a leave of absence without pay and then return to work. The next morning, my first e-mail is one of termination of employment with no explanation.

Accepting this fate, I decided I will wait until my cast is removed and then start looking for work. Approximately five days after my cast is removed, and when I awake in the morning, my neck feels like I have slept on it wrong. I make another appointment with the doctor. Now he is sending me for an MRI of my neck and spine. The MRI results come back and show that my C-5 and C-6 discs are herniated. By the time nightfall arrives, the ulnar nerve in my left arm is caught in the herniation. I pace the floor with tears streaming down my cheeks. The pain is excruciating, and there is no relief.

They send me to an orthopedic surgeon, who orders physical therapy to try and separate the discs and free the nerve. At this point, they don't know which ulnar nerve it is that has been caught in the herniation. More tests are ordered, where they try to isolate the nerve by injecting a solution around it to see if there is any pain relief afterward. You lie perfectly still on a table while they inject you. This procedure is performed three different times on different days. Finally, on the third try, they have isolated the nerve it is the number 6 ulnar. For about 15 minutes until the lidocaine wears off, I am pain-free. Slowly, it starts to return.

After nine months of pain, a decision is finally made to send me to a spine surgeon. I arrive at the surgeon's office feeling nervous, but the pain has gone on for so long that I am grateful to be here. He enters the office. I like him instantly; his smile lights up the room as he introduces himself and shakes my hand. After taking his X-rays and images, he shows me where the herniation is. He tells me that no amount of physical therapy would ever have released this nerve and informs me that his first available surgery date is in January. It is now October 2008. My eyes start to well up with tears, January seems so far away. He takes one look at me and calls the hospital to see if there is an operating room available on a Friday morning, his usual day off.

Upon returning, he informs me that he can do the surgery on November 14. I am so grateful and tell him that it is the second, best day of my life. He looks at me quizzically, so I tell him that is my son's birthday, considering this to be a good omen. Going home that afternoon, I breathe a little easier, knowing there is an end in sight. I need to start preparing. The surgeon told me that I could not be alone for at least eight weeks after surgery, and I won't be able to raise my arms above my head for that period.

I start to make phone calls. The first one is to Trisha. She will stay with me for the first six weeks, and a dear friend Heather will stay for the remaining weeks. Having never been in a hospital other than for the birth of my son, I'm not sure what to expect, and needles make me queasy.

Before my surgery date, my sister arrives, and a calm, peaceful feeling rushes over me. It makes me realize that being alone does have its pitfalls.

November 14 has arrived. We enter the hospital about 6 a.m. I am taken to prepare for surgery. The night shift is getting ready to leave as the day nurses are arriving. There is a lot of commotion, and the staff seems to be a little grumpy starting their day. I've changed into my hospital gown, and my vitals are taken. The nurse brings papers over for me to sign.

After about fifteen minutes go by, I can hear the surgeon as he enters the room. There is that great smile again, and everyone's mood seems to lighten. He pulls up a chair to sit next to me and explains the procedure and the risks involved. The only real risk seems to be that you could lose your voice; it could change to sound raspy (which could be sexy, I think). The reason for this is because they will enter through the front of my neck and move the vocal cords to perform the cervical spine fusion. A cadaver bone will be put in between the C-5 and C-6 discs with a metal plate and two titanium screws to hold it in place until the bone will become a part of my skeletal system.

They wheel me in for surgery, and when I awake, my sister is standing beside my bed. The first thing I ask her is if I sound like myself. She replies, "Exactly."

I feel fabulous for the first time in nine months. There is no pain running down my arm. I realize that I'm starving, and a headache is starting. The nurse tells me I can only have ice chips for the next 24 hours due to the risk of hurting the vocal cords or getting an infection. The surgery was nothing compared to what I have been through already.

David and his family come to visit. Sitting up, I'm chatting with them when the nurse comes in to give me some pain medication. I feel so good I tell her that nothing is needed. She starts flipping through the chart and asks, "Didn't you have cervical spine surgery this morning?" I tell her I did, but I have no pain. She shakes her head as she walks out.

Later that day, the surgeon comes in to see how I'm doing. A hard collar is around my neck to keep it straight and in an upright position for healing. After examining me, he explains that everything looks good, but the brace is too big, and a smaller custom-made one will have to be ordered. In the meantime, this is to be worn 24/7 for the next eight weeks to be removed only when I shower. I'm looking at my surgeon he has the most beautiful teeth; I feel a need to ask if those are his real teeth, they are so white and perfectly straight. He laughs out loud and answers, "Every last one of them."

The next day, I'm released to go home. Now, the healing process begins. The hard brace was starting to rub on my collar bone making it sore, so my sister made a soft piece out of a towel to wrap like a scarf around my shoulders and neck so that the brace rested on it. It worked quite well. I had to sleep propped up with pillows on my back; the collar still slipped around as I slept at night.

Trisha has another idea. The collar has an oval opening at the front. She takes my soft cotton underwear out of the drawer and decides to stuff a few of them inside the opening to keep it from slipping. It sounded brilliant at the time. I go to sleep quite peacefully, but sometime during the night, I wake up choking. The underwear has dislodged, putting pressure on my throat. Immediately, I start pulling them out one by one, tossing them everywhere. When my sister comes in the next morning, she sees them scattered across the room. We laugh at this! Not a good idea.

I'm not allowed to raise my arms above my head. So, for me to be able to take a shower, we place one of those plastic outdoor chairs in the shower, where I sit while my sister washes my hair for me. One thing about being sick or injured is that you learn to accept help. Which is something I was never very good at doing before this. My sister leaves after six weeks, and my dear friend flies in for the second shift. The weeks pass by, and after eight weeks I get to start wearing the soft collar brace which makes it much easier to sleep.

Upon returning to the surgeon after eight weeks for my check-up, everything looks good; the surgery was a success. I now get to wear a soft collar for two weeks which is much more comfortable than the hard version. Still, home recuperating, my left shoulder starts to hurt and becomes difficult to move. Once again, I am sitting in the doctor's office. Upon examining my shoulder, he tells me I have what is called frozen shoulder, which was caused by not using my left arm for about 11 months. He describes it as a piece of shrink wrap that needs to be broken apart. Physical therapy is ordered.

I am in physical therapy for the next eight weeks; not much progress has been made, and it's extremely painful. A friend informs me of a chiropractor who is coming to do a seminar in our city. He does energy healing, which might sound crazy, but at this point, I will try anything. We attend, and afterward, as I approach him, he looks directly at me and, puts his hand on my left shoulder. He does a movement like he is flicking something off. He finishes, asking me to raise my left arm above my head and then behind my back. OMG! The frozen shoulder is completely gone, never to return.

In leaving this chapter, I hope you will be open to alternative methods of healing. Whether it is naturopathic, osteopathic, chiropractic, acupuncture, or energy healing. There are so many new modalities that are available to enable us in our healing process. A surgeon is needed at times, but also go within yourself and believe. The human body is an amazing structure, housing our spiritual being. It is in our best interest to care for it as best we can.

The Blue Wings of the Dragonfly

SUN-KISSED GRAPES

"LIVE in each season as it passes; breathe the air, drink the drink, taste the fruit, and resign yourself to the influence of the Earth."

Henry David Thoreau

Morning is here, the sky so blue it hurts my eyes if I glance too long at it. I feel the warmth on my face and arms as I plant flowers, one of my favorite things to do. The soil is cool to the touch, and I dig deeper to create the space for my flowers. You can smell the earth; each flower has its scent, the fragrances almost mesmerizing. Gardening helps to ground me, to feel connected. There is an exchange of energies. I am getting as much from this as the plants and flowers are. They bring a smile to my face, and when they bloom in all their glorious colors of bright reds, yellows, oranges, and blues and the green of the leaves. I'm reminded of a new box of Crayola crayons. Who didn't love the smell of a new box of crayons, and the wonderful blank canvas set in front of you to fill with your imagination? Every picture tells a story. Life is like that blank canvas; we color it in as we go.

We all need to connect with nature. A walk in the woods, the smell of the pine needles drifting in the cool air of the forest. A stroll along the beach, feeling the sand and water between your toes as the waves create a frothy, bubbly effect coming to shore. You can smell the salt in the air, almost taste it. The shells and sand dollars are left lingering behind, waiting for us to pick up to add to our collection.

Recalling running through the Concord grape vineyards, stopping to catch my breath, I see the sun warming the grapes as they glisten with moisture. Reaching over and picking a bunch, I revel in their juicy sweetness. I remember the brightly colored fall leaves. Gathering the leaves, to press them in between the pages of a book to dry and preserve for a future date. Picking up chestnuts off the sidewalks that had fallen during the night. They were a rich auburn color. Such wonderful treasures indeed.

The night skies in rural New York are jet black thanks to a complete lack of city light pollution. Stars in the sky appear to be diamonds. On special nights, however, when the full moon would appear on newly fallen snow, its light would reflect a prism-affect in millions of ice crystals. Walking outside, I could see a glittering rainbow shining across the virgin snow. It was a spectacle that dazzled the eyes, and I remember it vividly.

The earth grounds us; brings us back to ourselves. What are you doing to connect? It's the simple things that count the most in our lives. It's easy to take them for granted, so be sure and stop once in a while and breathe. Pay attention to the world around you. Many of us get caught up in our daily routines and responsibilities. Don't... STOP! Take the time. We never know if this is our last moment, our last breath on earth. No regrets. Enjoy!

MY SON

"You are my Sunshine ...
You make me ... Happy
You'll never know dear,
how much I Love You!
... Please don't take My Sunshine ...
away."

Jimmie Davis

I have always said from the moment he was born that my son was the best thing that ever happened to me. Nothing is like the birth of a child. His first breath took mine away. The moment I held him in my arms and his eyes met mine; I felt a sense of recognition, a connection so deep, I could feel it in my soul. His life gave new meaning to my own.

I have always been a caregiver, but this was extraordinary, having someone who needs you and truly loves you. Children love unconditionally. For me, it meant far more than that. It brought a sense of peace and a meaning to my life that I had been running away from for a long time. It brought forgiveness.

His smile, his sweetness. Loving, kind, honest, intelligent, stubborn, and strong. David was always a quiet child, an only child. As the years passed, I watched him grow. Remembering his high school football games, his first prom date, the broken relationships, his college days. On the day he moved out of the house, I thought my heart would break. I stood in the entryway of our home and just cried. He held me for a moment.

One day he came home and told me he was going to ask Nicole to marry him, wanting to know if I would help him pick out the engagement ring; my heart smiled. He wanted to surprise her and worried that she might already have a clue because he had shared it with one of her best friends, so we devised a plan. He would take her to dinner and then come by the house afterward. Darryl and I would create a romantic setting in the backyard.

Having this task, we sprang into action. We started blowing up pink and white balloons all day to set in the yard. Candle tea lights lined a low wall in our yard around the patio. I purchased champagne, wine glasses, and a crystal vase with two dozen pink roses, her favorite color. We had drawn the shades on the windows, concealing the outdoors.

He called me from the men's restroom at the restaurant to say they were leaving. We hurried to light all the candles outside; a slight breeze was blowing, but we were determined. They arrived, and then he asked her to go outside and swing on the patio. I think she thought it was rude since they had just arrived, but as he opened the back door, I caught a smile on her face. We let them have their time, afterward neighbors and friends came to join the celebration.

A year later they were married. The wedding was perfect except for the fact that my mother and Darryl had both passed before this wonderful event. I'm sure they were there in spirit, not wanting to miss this special time. We all knew they were there in our hearts.

My son is an amazing father. He adopted my Nicole's little girl, who was seven at the time. I was very proud of him, and three years later, my granddaughter was born. Then, two-and-a-half years later, my grandson was born. Watching them grow, reminds me of the innocence of childhood and how precious that time is. Their lives are busy but happy. Today, he still sings the same song to them that I sang to him as a child: "You Are My Sunshine."

BABY OF MINE

"I cannot think of any need in a childhood as strong as the need for a father's protection."

Sigmund Freud

The year is 1970. I am a freshman in high school, falling head over heels for a junior in my school. Patrick was my first love. Kind, sweet, and intelligent, he came from a good family. Best of all, though, he wasn't in any of my father's classes.

We started dating and were inseparable. I needed a loving male figure in my life since my father was never there for me emotionally. There was a group of us couples who would do everything together. I always seemed older than my age, mainly because of the responsibilities I had taken on as a child. By my junior year, we were having sex but always used protection. He was in his first year of college and came home on the weekends. One month, I failed to get my period. We both knew that trouble was ahead. Trying to figure things out, we didn't tell anyone for a while. We made a joint decision that we would marry and live in an upstairs apartment of a friend. He would get a job and continue with night school, and all would be well.

My dreams were like glass shattering into many pieces, falling in all directions. I finally told my mother, and she held me while I cried. She would be the one to break the news to my father. I knew this was not going to go well. He had a terrible temper, and when he drank it was even worse. That night I could hear yelling and screaming upstairs as I lay in my bed, frightened and unable to sleep. Patrick would tell his parents that same night.

The next morning, I didn't go to school. My mom took me to a doctor to confirm the pregnancy. I was more than three months pregnant. That night everyone pretended things were normal; we had dinner, I did my homework, and nothing was said. As I crawled into bed, I remember talking to the baby, saying everything will be all right. As time passed, my father cried with my mom sitting on the sofa next to him, trying to plead my case. My father kept saying that he couldn't have his daughter be pregnant, no one at school could know, as it would ruin his precious reputation. In the meantime, my boyfriend's parents were very supportive. They had decided that we could live with them, and they'd help raise the baby while he finished college.

I was now five months pregnant. At least I think that's how far along I was. I was losing track of time. My father had made his decision. I could not have this baby. He had my cousin Faye track down a doctor in Buffalo who was performing abortions, which were illegal at that time.

I didn't want an abortion. I wanted my baby. I started crying hysterically. Every part of my being hurt. Physically, emotionally and spiritually.

The next night, Patrick came over with his parents to talk with mine. I'd never seen my father so angry as he was that night. He had been drinking. He grabbed my boyfriend by the throat and pushed him up against the wall; all the while his parents were yelling, trying to free their son from his grip. My father would listen to nothing. He told them to get the hell out of his house, or he would file charges for statutory rape since I was a minor, and he wasn't. I hated my father at that moment!

Everyone left. I was sobbing; my mom tried to comfort me. My dad was so out of control that he grabbed a lamp from the table and smashed it to the floor. Somewhere in the background, Trisha was there, not understanding what was going on. I lay in bed that night, still crying and, rubbing my stomach to soothe myself. Things quieted upstairs and around 3 a.m. my mother came quietly down the stairs. She held me and told me that if I wanted to keep my baby, she would take all of us kids, there were four of us now and leave my father. I couldn't do that to them. The wrath he would bring on all of us would be more than I could bear.

A couple of days later, my father drove us to Buffalo for a consult with the doctor. I sat there as he explained the procedure, telling my parents that at this stage of pregnancy they could lose us both and it was very risky. I looked at my father, pleading with my eyes in the hope that he would change his mind, but he didn't even flinch. It cut like a knife through my heart. Not only did he not want my baby, but he didn't care if I lived or died. The appointment was set.

Faye picked me up the next morning and that night was spent in a hotel room with her. My mom would return in the morning to be with me for the abortion. My emotions were all over the place. I was sad but also afraid, thinking perhaps I wouldn't survive. Well, at least I would be with my baby then.

Morning arrived, and my mom was there. I was admitted to the hospital and brought up to a room. Putting on my hospital gown, I lay on the bed. The doctor came in and asked if we were ready. No words were spoken. He pulled out a large needle that was put in my belly. It hurt a lot. He explained it was a type of saline solution. Labor would start soon after that, but the baby would not be alive. Tears streamed down my face. I screamed in pain for nine hours, my mother wiping my forehead with a cold cloth. She never left my side and held my hand the whole time.

Somewhere around 4 p.m., I was told to start pushing. A nurse came in with a metal bucket, and soon after, I heard the most horrible sound in my life, one I will never forget; the sound of my baby dropping in a bucket. Dead, no breath of air, no crying. Another nurse came in and immediately tried to calm me, saying my daughter was in heaven now. The doctor followed, and, after checking on me, said I could go home the next morning. I had lived, but at the same time, I wished I had died. I'm so sorry I couldn't save you, baby. So sorry, baby of mine.

My memory for the rest of that year was lost. I don't even remember the car ride home the next morning. I have tried to recall, but nothing comes. I want to ask my mother for details that seem to be hidden in the realms of my subconscious, but she has been gone for 16 years now, and I never got the chance to ask her. Perhaps it is best that I don't remember. Eventually, the baby's father and I got back together, but it didn't last very long. Neither of us could get past the loss and to see each other was a constant reminder of it.

BAD BLACK HABITS

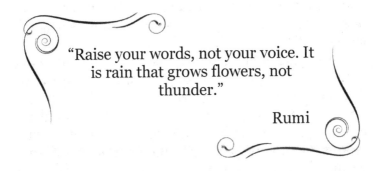

"Raise your words, not your voice. It is rain that grows flowers, not thunder."

Rumi

The decision for myself and my siblings to attend Catholic school from kindergarten through the eighth grade was made because we lived within walking distance to the school from our home. Nonni (Italian for grandma) was very pleased, as she was a devout Catholic. All four of us siblings were eventually there at the same time. We wore uniforms; plaid skirts and white blouses with black and white saddle shoes. Since I love color, this was not off to a very good start. My mother was a very good seamstress, and I loved all the dresses she would make for me.

The nuns, or sisters as they were called, had long black robes with large white collars and a type of hood that covered their heads and hair. All you could see were their faces and hands. A set of rosary beads was always to be found somewhere attached to the garment. I found this scary looking; all I could think of was Halloween where everyone was in costume. The nuns did not seem like very nice people to me. All rules were to be obeyed, and if not, a punishment of some sort was sure to follow.

One particular day, we were practicing our penmanship, and the sisters would walk up and down the aisles looking over our shoulders to see how we were doing. A boy in my class seemed to be struggling with his writing. Instead of nicely talking to him and showing him what he was doing wrong, I heard a loud voice and then a cracking sound made by the wooden ruler in her hands. It landed straight across his knuckles; then there was crying. I winced just thinking about it. You could tell he was embarrassed, but she didn't care.

She marched him down the hallway to the Mother Superior's office, the sounds echoing in the halls. I had a new fear of that wooden ruler and the nun wielding it. My penmanship to this day remains beautiful.

Arithmetic problems were often done on the blackboard. Math was a subject I never loved. Being called up to the front of the class was not a fond memory for me. I'd have to write the equation on the chalkboard. As I stared at the piece of white chalk in my hand, my mind would go blank as I looked at the arithmetic problem on the blackboard. The harsh words kept coming until I could feel the burn of the salty tears streaming down my face. I'd then be ordered back to my seat, feeling so ashamed of myself. What a joy Catholic school was NOT!

I was in third grade when Trisha started kindergarten. It felt good to have someone else there whom I knew so well. At recess time, we could go to the windows looking out over the playground, which happened to be the kindergarten classroom, and I would wave and smile to my sister. When my brother started a couple of years later, he would always cry when my sister and I would drop him off at the kindergarten door. My sister and I were told that at recess we were not allowed near those windows because my brother Jim would start to cry again if he could see us. In later years, he would tell me that he always felt abandoned because all the other kids were waving and smiling at their sisters and brothers, but we never came.

Sitting in class on a beautiful sunny day looking out the window which faced Central Avenue, I see a little boy running as fast as he can across the green lawn. He's heading for our street. I think he looks familiar. I realize it's my brother, who had somehow managed to escape the kindergarten room. He was being chased by Sister Peter, who was about six feet tall and weighed at least 200 pounds. She was fast on his trail. About then, I hear one of the kids in class say, "Isn't that your brother?" Sister Peter caught up with him and tackles him to the ground. I thought she would crush him, but he appeared unscathed from the whole ordeal. It was his first escape attempt but wouldn't be his last.

The only fond memories I had during those years were of Sister Monica. She was so sweet and, had the prettiest face, always smiling. Her sister and her brother-in-law came to visit, and her sister held me on her lap. I remember her sister saying that she wished, I could go home with them. The other good memory was in eighth grade. A science fair was held every year at the school, and I took first place. A photo was published in our hometown newspaper showing me with Father Bernardo and my project with a beautiful blue ribbon attached. A proud moment. The next year, public high school. Yes!

THE SWING IN THE BASEMENT

"Innocence, once lost. Can never be regained. Darkness, once gazed upon, can never be lost."

John Milton

We were moving into our new house that my father had designed and built. I had my room upstairs painted pink, my favorite color. The first pet I ever had was a cat named Silky. On my way home from kindergarten, a stray dog followed me (with a little coaxing on my part, of course). Mom said I could keep him if no one claimed him in the next couple of days. The dog was good company at night in my room. As a child, I was quiet and shy. I was an only child for more than four years, and quite content. My mother was very loving. She had a beautiful smile. I remember her smiling at me a lot.

My father built a swing in the basement for me so while mom was doing laundry or sewing (her favorite hobby), and through the cold winter months, I would still have a place to swing. I loved to sing and would put on the old record player and sing to my favorite Disney album. My favorite song was "Someday My Prince Will Come." I'd sing so loud that sometimes my mom would come down the stairs to tell me to be quieter because often, my dad was trying to take a nap.

I was so happy when I was on my swing. Little did I know that one day that basement would hold a different memory for me.

During the summer as I stepped outside, I could feel the splendor of the sunshine on my face and, the smell of the fields across the street. There was a huge pond within walking distance of our home, just across the railroad tracks that were well-hidden behind the lush trees and landscape. I remember getting a bucket and going next door to get my best friend, Paul. We would go to the pond and gather pollywogs and bring them home. I would put them in a plastic pool that dad had set up in the backyard, so I could feed them and watch them grow, slowly developing legs and feet and eventually becoming these minuscule little frogs. It's unbelievable, the wonder of creation. I knew even then we were all connected in some way.

REMEMBERING CHICKENS

"Sometimes you will never know the
true value of a moment until it
becomes a memory."

Michelle Collero

For me, growing up Easter was always a fun time.
My father built a long island bar in our family
room. On Easter morning all four of our baskets
would be lined up on the counter, each one
wrapped with a different color of cellophane: pink,
purple, green or yellow, with a bright ribbon tied
at the top. I loved the colors of Easter.

We would all wake up early and peer into our
baskets delighting in what we could see through
the cellophane.

Milk chocolate and white chocolate bunnies,
assorted jelly beans, marshmallow chicks, speckled
eggs, chocolate carrots and somewhere in the
basket was one toy or book, usually hidden in the
plastic grass so you couldn't see it. The rule was
that we had to wait until mom and dad were up.
We waited patiently, excited to see all that was
inside our baskets. When we opened them, the air

was permeated with the sweet smell of candy. My personal favorites were the white chocolate bunny and the marshmallow chicks. Biting into the soft marshmallow, I could feel the sugary coating melting in my mouth and the sweet taste of the marshmallow to follow. Everyone had a favorite flavor of jelly bean. Mine were the pink ones, grapefruit I think. My father loved the black licorice ones, and we would always save those for him.

We'd search under the brightly colored straw to find our toys. Mine was usually a Barbie doll or a set of Barbie clothes or accessories. Sometimes there were jacks to play with, or my brothers would get those small airplanes made of balsa wood to send sailing through the house. I remember they also had these little plastic soldiers attached to a parachute, that they'd send up in the air and watch as they came floating down.

Later in the day, my dad would pick up my nonni, who always made a cake shaped like a lamb with white frosting and shaved coconut flakes for the fur. The eyes, nose, and mouth were made of jelly beans she had cut and placed. We also ate honey-glazed ham and mashed potatoes, and, of course, lots and lots of candy.

One Easter was very special. Upon awakening, our parents were carrying a cardboard box into the room, and to my delight, there were eight live baby chicks. They were yellow, blue and pink. The feed store would have them dyed which would soon wear off. I was so excited to have these baby chicks! I'm sure my mom thought that the chicks would not live long, but I was on a mission determined to keep them alive. At night they were brought downstairs to my room in the cardboard box. Taking one of my nightstand lamps and placing it in the middle of the box, I covered the top of the lampshade with tin foil, that way all the heat from the light would go down into the box.

The chicks would huddle together under the warmth and every morning at 2 a.m. they would wake up wanting to eat. I'd climb out of bed to feed them and make sure they drank some water and then fall back to sleep. In the morning I would bring the box back upstairs to the kitchen, so my mom could keep a watchful eye on them while I was in school. A few months passed and one morning, to our surprise, a chicken flew out of the box and onto the kitchen table. My mother did not look happy. "That's it," she said, "those chickens have to go."

I was fighting back the tears, asking her why? She was not much of an animal lover, not in the house anyway. My father said not to worry because one of the teachers at the high school lived on a farm and had chickens, so he would ask him to take them. The next Saturday, my dad and I drove out to Mr. Bixby's house, and he brought me to the barn where he was raising his chickens, assuring me they would not be killed but used to get fresh eggs. When I started high school the following year, he would bring me a dozen eggs every once in a while. That made me happy.

Oddly enough, years later my mom would talk fondly about going to her aunt Nellie's farm in Alabama as a child where they had chickens. She started collecting all kinds of decorative chickens. I even made a couple for her out of ceramic. They were everywhere in her kitchen. After she passed Trisha and I couldn't bear to part with them, so we packed them in a box, and my sister still has them packed away. To this day when I see something with a chicken or rooster, I always think of my mother and smile.

On sultry summer days, we would gather in the backyard to enjoy a cool afternoon breeze. Inevitably, someone would suggest ice cream! That would cause a flurry of activity. Getting the cream from the local dairy, fresh strawberries, sugar, and ice to combine all the necessary ingredients into an ancient hand-cranked ice cream maker then labor mightily to churn out the finished product. Each of us would take a turn, and it seemed to take forever. Finally, the time would arrive when the ice cream was ready. As you know, there is nothing like the deliciousness of homemade strawberry ice cream on a hot summer day.

THE ATRIUM, MY SANCTUARY

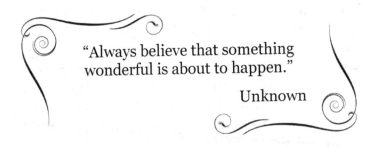

"Always believe that something wonderful is about to happen."

Unknown

One day, I knew something had changed. Where was Daddy? Mom seemed to be spending a lot of time away from home. Nonni is taking care of us during the day. Mom told me that Daddy was very sick, and we would have to spend some time away from home. I started crying. I didn't want to leave my home. I can still remember the feeling in the pit of my stomach wondering if we would be back soon, and why this was happening. I was seven years old at the time.

We were split up for a while, so my mom could care for my dad. My sister and I went to the Franks' house. They were good friends with my parents although at the time I wasn't sure who they were. It was very disturbing. My brother Jim went to Mr. and Mrs. Falcone's house. Mr. Falcone was my dad's friend and plumber. My youngest brother Douglas stayed with Nonni.

I remember this huge area with glass on all four sides in the center of the Franks' home. Inside it was like a miniature forest. There were a lot of birds, and some of their colors were amazing! There were shades of turquoise, yellow, orange, red, and blue. The tiny finches, parakeets, and canaries were always busy flying from one branch to the next eating, drinking, and chirping. Come nightfall they; would pick a spot to settle in puff out their chests and be sound asleep gathering energy for the next day. I was mesmerized. To this day birds still, have a tranquil effect on me.

I would cry softly at night. I missed my mom, my dad, my bed, my home. I wrote letters to my dad while he was in the hospital. Hoping they would make him feel better. Later he told me that they helped to make him smile. A memory about an afternoon in the basement of our home came to mind. I thought about a particular day in that cellar. I had come home from school anxious to get on my swing, so I headed for the basement stairs. I heard my dad yelling. Going down one step at a time, I stopped halfway down. My Mom was trying to help him up. He had a rope around his neck and was on the cement floor. A chair with a broken leg was there next to my swing, which was partially moving back and forth, hanging by one chain. With all the confusion and noise going on, I continued down the stairs and Mom's eyes locked on mine. "What is Daddy doing on the floor?"

Stumbling and crying she eventually got him up the stairs and into bed. I would later learn he had tried to hang himself that day. I no longer wanted to swing in the basement. The innocence of childhood was taken from me. I suddenly had a barrage of questions that I would ask myself though at the time I did not fully comprehend the severity of the situation.

One day Mom came to pick us up. I was so excited to be going home!

C. Lee Roggeman

Dear Dad
I Love you
and I hope you
come back
soon and when
you do we can
play Games
and we have been
saying prayers
at Night Good By
Daddy Over
and we are
haveing a test
Tomorrow
GoodBy.

122

From Cindy

Dear dad

I Love you

we had our test

today it was easy

for me and I hope
you Get better soon

and dad Jimmy
sure was a Messy
maker I cleaned
The deck for mommy
I've been a Good girl
and evry Thing
was Good forc

Lunch and we've been
saying a prayer. For
you

NONNI

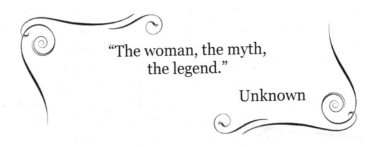

"The woman, the myth,
the legend."

Unknown

My Nonni came from Sicily, Italy to Ellis Island at the age of three. Her family settled in New York in a tiny town called Dunkirk, named after its sister city in France. Her parents owned a small mercantile store. When I think of her, I remember she was a force to be reckoned with, independent, and strong. Creative, and she loved her flowers. She was not what I would call a typical grandmother. I don't remember hugs and kisses, but if you had done something she approved of, there was always a sense of pride in her eyes.

She was always cooking. Every Saturday she'd make chicken soup. On Sundays, she made spaghetti sauce with meatballs, sausage, and a pork hock thrown in for sweetness; pies; and the most delicious bread I have ever tasted in my life. I would watch her knead the dough, then roll it into what would become perfect sandwich-sized rolls.

We would chuckle because when she was letting the dough rise, she would cover it first with a towel and then one of the afghans she had knitted with squares of all different colors. Perhaps that was her secret ingredient. If you were lucky to stay over that Saturday night, in the morning, she would make fried bread, taking the dough and patting it out with her hands to fry in her iron skillet and then sprinkling it with powdered sugar. We would eat it warm right from the pan. It was so incredibly yummy. My mouth still waters, just thinking of it.

She always had a garden and grew most of her vegetables. I remember helping to pick some of the tomatoes, peas, and corn on the cob. The smell of tomato growing on the vine was heavenly. Sweet raw corn was also one of my favorites. Nonni always had garlic for cooking, and she would say "a clove of garlic a day keeps the doctor away." Her favorite perfume was Avon's Rose Water. Therefore she always smelled of garlic and rosewater. An odd combination, and to this day, it still reminds me of her.

On many weekends, a bunch of the cousins would stay overnight. There might be six or eight of us. She always had cold Orange Crush to drink and buttery popcorn with lots of salt. Her original home was by a railroad track, and, at night, as I lay there falling asleep to the sounds of the trains going by with whistles blowing, it felt safe and serene. In the morning, when it was cold, she would put the radiator on, and we would gather round to warm ourselves. On her porch were hammocks she made from material she had sewn and a swing my father had built. We would rock the new grandbabies to sleep in the hammocks on a nice summer afternoon, eventually all taking naps.

Every Sunday afternoon my dad, mom, sister, brothers, and Nonni would all pile into the car for our Sunday drive in the country. Passing the farms along the way, we'd see the cows grazing. She would always wave out the window, saying, "Hello, girls!" and we would all giggle in the back seat. We'd always stop at the Italian store, with its huge selection of fresh bread and confections. Freezer display cases were brimming with ice creams, gelatos, and spumoni. My favorite. Another had meats, hard/dried sausage, olive and cheese displays. Mom and Dad would make their selections to take home with us to eat later that day with Nonni's scrumptious bread.

A few doors down was what we called "the squeeze cup store," which sold Italian ice in these little paper cups that you had to squeeze to get all the flavored ice out. It also had a wonderful candy display behind a large glass case. We were each allowed to pick out two pieces of candy. Mine was usually lipstick candy and those little brightly colored dots on a piece of paper. My brothers would choose the candy cigarettes and bubble gum cigars and my sister the candy necklaces. Upon bringing Nonni home, it never failed she would turn as she was getting out of the car and say, "Thanks for the buggy ride," leaving us laughing and shaking our heads.

Other times she was embarrassing. Like when she would get a paper bag and a weed digger and go around to the neighbors' yards collecting all the dandelion greens before they would flower and come back to make a huge dandelion salad. Eeww, so bitter! Or, when the circus came to town, and she'd push Douglas in the stroller, her little shovel, and bucket in tow, going behind the tents collecting elephant dung. She swore by it, saying it made the best fertilizer for her garden. We could at least run away, but my youngest brother was stuck with the smell in the stroller behind him. It's something we continue to tease him about to this day.

I also remember her watching Lawrence Welk and all the bubbles. She loved that music. Her bay window in the living room was filled with violets, some of the largest I have ever seen. She was quite proud of those. She taught me how to crochet, and I would sit for hours at home making my afghans. She was a seamstress for the Van Rault Company for many years. She always made the gorgeous christening gowns for all the grandchildren. She was very religious, a bond we didn't share. I was spiritual like my mother. My father, though he started off religious, would become agnostic over the years, always saying this was hell right here on Earth. My grandfather died when my nonni was 50 years old. She never remarried and never learned how to drive, preferring to walk everywhere.

She lived in her own home until the age of 96, when she had to be moved to an assisted living facility, She wasn't happy, longing for her flower and vegetable gardens. Eventually, she adjusted, and my Aunt Lou would find her on the porch, rocking, and knitting. My father was gone long before then. She said a parent should never outlive her children. One day after her lunch, she laid down to take a nap and passed away in her sleep at 100 years of age. Hers was a simple and happy life. Material things didn't matter to her. She had grown up in the depression era and found joy in the little things in life.

THE BEGINNING OF A SPIRITUAL JOURNEY

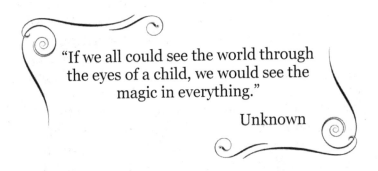

"If we all could see the world through the eyes of a child, we would see the magic in everything."

Unknown

Dad was still sick. I started to learn how to cook and do the laundry, also helping to take care of my brothers and sister, so that Mom could have more time with dad. He cried a lot, and always seemed so sad. Eventually, that time passed. Happier times were ahead, or so I thought. My mom was very spiritual. Almost every Saturday she would take me to Lily Dale Assembly, which is the oldest spiritual community in the United States. It was this quaint little village along Cassadaga Lake about 15 minutes from our home. Every year, from June through August, they would hold what was called Summer Session.

The homes are a unique Victorian-era style, with wrap-around porches and painted in lovely pastel colors, reminiscent of a postcard.

We would walk the grounds through the tall pine trees. You could feel the energy. The Divine Source was all around. There was also a very old pet cemetery, and I would love to go and read the names of the animals that had passed on. We used to go from one house to another for a reading of some kind. Some of the people were psychics, empaths, Tarot card readers, and astrologers. Guest speakers from all over the world would fly in to share their knowledge, and I would listen intently.

I became fascinated with that whole world and how we can connect with our loved ones even after they have left the earth plane. It was very comforting in a way. I knew that one day I would share what I had learned long ago, even before this life. In particular, I was captivated with astrology. It seemed like I had an inner knowing and a fascination with the stars and planets.

Eager to learn what it all meant, I started taking classes in Astrology. It was like tapping into something within. Through Astrology I gained so much knowledge about myself and others, certain traits and characteristics became clear when I had a chart in my hands. It was all numbers. Math creates each unique birth chart, and like snowflakes every chart was different. The interpretation was the important part. I would learn to shut out the outside world and revel in the stars and planets, tuning into their vibration. I knew there was so much more out there, unlimited possibilities of discovery.

When I was young, I always gravitated toward the grown-ups. My aunts would come by, and we would all sit around the kitchen table drinking coffee or tea. My Aunt Mae would have us drink our coffee or tea without sugar or cream, so we could learn to read the coffee grounds or tea leaves left in our cup. She had a whole ritual where you would turn your cup upside down with your left hand and let it dry on a paper towel. We would then turn it over, and she would show me all the people, animals, and mountains in the cup. All have a significant meaning, and you could weave a story by what you see. One day, I was disturbed by what I saw in my cup. A change was coming.

IN THE SILENCE

"I think 99 times and I find nothing,
I stop thinking, swim in silence, and
the truth comes to me."

Albert Einstein

It's 1967 now. My father was ill again and was taken to the hospital. I didn't understand what was wrong. This time, though, Mom would let me go to see him with her. The hospital was very unsettling; as we walked through the corridors, the smells were very peculiar and unfamiliar. There were lots of people milling about the hallways. Some seemed very strange in an odd sort of way. It was very disturbing. They were talking to themselves or to someone I couldn't see. One man startled me as I was walking by him. He turned and shouted, "I am Superman, and I can fly!"

It seemed like it took forever, but then I saw him, my dad. I was so glad to see him. I started running straight to him, and he gave me a big hug. He told me not to pay attention to the other people, and that he wasn't like that, he was normal.

In the days that followed, I took on more responsibility at home. I learned that my father was bipolar and manic and that he was an alcoholic. At the time, I didn't realize or even comprehend what all of that meant. I would eventually find out.

I learned how precious life was. How could anyone be so sad and unable to find their way back? When I am meditating, I hear or sense something telling me it's complicated. The conscious and subconscious are connected in many ways. My dad chose his journey as I have chosen mine, but I have found ways to be happy and to find joy in life. It took some time. For the most part, I was always positive and tried to see the best in people.

My father elected to suffer mentally and physically although now I know that alcoholism is a disease. In the end, he was alone and then he was gone all too early. The father I needed was never fully present. I had to find my inner strength, always listening to my guides. They would help me to relax when I was anxious.

Trust in the process. Surrender to it for when you do, life becomes so much easier, and things will fall into place. Be flexible; plans rarely go as you expect. There is a purpose, though. Through the divine, you can find yourself. Be open and accepting to follow the path to your true potential. Let go of what is no longer needed or unnecessary in your life. Keep what is beneficial. Remember the good times.

We are here for such a short time on this earth plane. Make the most of it! Enjoy life itself. The sun on your face. The sand beneath your toes. Rain at the end of a hot day. The taste of different foods. Visit foreign countries. Learn about the people. Find your passion. Very few people ever experience that. Why do you ask? Part of it is our programming, but we can work on changing that. Let go of ego and allow life to show you the way. Feel with your heart, not your mind. Get out of your head. In the silence is where I find the most peace. The stillness allows me to connect with my spirit, with my guides, and it is there that I can hear my heartbeat and feel connected to all the energies around me and within.

C. Lee Roggeman

MY FIRST WAKE

"It's the little moments together that make the best memories forever."

Unknown

I was five years old. Mom informed me we were going to ride on an airplane to Alabama, where she was born. I would get to meet aunts, uncles, and cousins from her side of the family that I had never met before. I was excited and nervous. She was sad; I saw her crying. I wondered why?

She was busy packing that night, and I watched as she loaded clothes into the suitcase. Phone calls were coming in. She smiled at me, but I knew she wasn't her happy self. As I boarded the plane the next morning, I was amazed at how big it was. Dad and Mom sat me between them. The engines roared, and a man's voice came over the loudspeaker. Dad told me it was the pilot flying the plane. Before long, we were in the air. Mom lets me sit on her lap and look out the window. We were up in the clouds. The nice lady on the plane asked if I wanted to hand out gum to all the other passengers. I was so excited to be handing out gum to everyone. She walked behind me as I gave each person a little box with two squares of Chiclets gum in it. I was smiling the whole time, and all the people said hello to me. It was a good day! I took out my crayons and coloring book, and Mom read stories to me.

The plane landed, and we waited for a carousel going around and around to deliver our luggage from the plane. Pretty soon, a man came up to my mother and called her by name and then they were hugging. "This is your Uncle Norm," Mom said.

We loaded into his car, and I fell fast asleep. The next thing I knew, I was in a strange bedroom on an unfamiliar bed. Starting to cry, I called out for my mom. Two teenagers came running in. I continued to cry. They told me my mom and dad would be back soon though I still wasn't comforted. A little dog was barking, and my cousins placed her on the bed next to me. She was licking me all over. Temporarily, I was amused. Then panic set in again. Where were they?

One of my cousins went to a closet door and opened it. Upon seeing stacks of comic books, my eyes grew as big as saucers. I got off the bed to have a look. There were all kinds of them. I picked several out, and they sat down beside me and began to read. I heard the door open and my mom and dad's familiar voices. I ran to my mom. "Where were you?" I asked. "Why did you leave me?"

She sat down and tried to explain to me that my grandfather, who she referred to as "Big Daddy," had died. I was trying to piece this all together. Having never met him, I didn't fully understand but felt sad for my mom.

Morning came, and everyone was getting ready. Mom said we were going to Big Daddy's house. Arriving, we got out of the car and entered the house. So many people, relatives of my mom trying to talk to me all of them strangers, people I had never met before. I hid behind my mom. Then I saw him. He was lying in this huge box that resembled a bed, but it was sitting on a table. His eyes were shut, and he was not moving. His skin looked milky white; his hair was brown and curly like mine.

It felt like a dream. I found a small wooden rocking chair, set it in the middle of the room, and sat myself down. Everyone was dressed in black. Some of the people were crying; some were laughing and telling stories. Dad brought me a plate of food, but I wasn't hungry. He said these were my mom's brothers and sisters and their children, my cousins. Mom was smiling more, and she seemed happy to see them. An older lady came up to me and knelt down beside me with her face right in front of mine, "You must be Gaynell's daughter." I slapped her across the face, and before I knew it, Mom had scooped me up in her arms, and never let go the rest of the day. Yes! She was the wicked stepmother.

I had grown fond of the little dog, who kept me company at night, sleeping by my side. Her name was Chi Chi. We were getting ready to leave a couple of days later. I started crying, not wanting to leave the dog. My uncle said, "You can take her with you if your mom and dad say it's OK." I looked at them anxiously, and they agreed. A few days later, we left with Chi Chi in a carrier. She was my first dog. In the days that followed, Mom seemed quieter than usual. I guess she was missing her dad. I remember thinking that I would be very sad to not have my dad or mom with me. One night, at bedtime, Mom told me that she would always be with me in spirit no matter what might happen. It helped to ease my thoughts.

MY MOTHER'S
STILLBORN CHILD

"You were a part of me for
just a little while. I grieve because I'll
never see the magic in your smile."

Unknown

The year was 1961. I was six years old. I remember my mother being pregnant. He would have been her fourth child. She seemed to be very happy about it. She was always quietly optimistic. We would take turns rubbing her belly, anxiously awaiting the arrival of our new sibling. One day after coming home from the doctor, Mom seemed very sad. She was crying. When I asked her, what was wrong her reply was, "Nothing honey it will be OK."

I didn't know how much time had passed, but one day Dad took her to the hospital. When they came home the next day, I knew something was wrong. Where was the baby?

Mom had been crying again. She sat me down and said the baby didn't make it. What? My six-year-old mind was trying to comprehend this. "So where did the baby go," I asked. She said, "The baby is in a better place now; that he wasn't healthy." Time passed and soon after mom was pregnant again. This time she came home, from the hospital with our new, healthy baby brother Douglas. She was smiling again.

Years later, as we sat down over a cup of tea, I asked her what had happened. She explained that at some point very late in the pregnancy the baby's heart had stopped beating and she felt no more movement. In the sixties, they had her carry the baby to term even though she knew he was already gone. It seemed so barbaric to me having to carry a baby that you knew was already gone. How does a mother cope with that? To that day her grief and sadness remained, as tears welled up in her eyes. I held her as she wept once more. The loss of a child in whatever manner is the hardest loss. Not even time can heal that wound. It eases up but returns at moments when you least expect it, like a lightning bolt! It's tucked away in our subconscious. Out of reach but fragments of tiny bits of residue, remain.

JAZZ

"When you are sorrowful look again in your heart, and you shall see that in truth you are weeping, for that which has been your delight."

Khalil Gibran

On June 14, 2017, my beloved dog Jazz (Jasmine) had to be euthanized. She had been with me for 13 years, and she was a constant companion after the death of my husband in 2005.

I saw an advertisement in the paper for a 10-week-old Lhasapoo. An elderly couple was looking to find a loving home for this puppy. Having just lost their dog of sixteen years and wanting to fill that void, they chose this little rescue dog. After two weeks they realized that a puppy was more than they could handle. Remembering how much work a puppy could be.

I called and got directions to their house. Upon arriving, they opened the door and led me into the kitchen. There she was, sitting, this tiny fluff ball of fur. Solid black the only white I could see were the whites of her eyes when they would dart back and forth. I loved her the moment I set eyes on her. Playfully coming to me, so sweet and gentle. She was mine.

Riding home in the car that day, she rested on my lap. Wondering myself what I had gotten into buying a puppy. It turned out to be one of the best decisions of my life. Jazz brought life back into the house. Running back and forth, chasing her favorite soft green ball. Making me laugh as she would slide across the tile floor. At night, her favorite spot was at the foot of my bed, and in that silence, it was comforting to know she was there. In the morning when I would first start to open my eyes, she would crawl slowly up to my side to get some extra cuddling time. Her fur felt soft as a cotton ball.

Jazz grew to about fourteen pounds, but now she had white fur shaped like an inverted triangle under her chin, and with her red collar, it almost looked like she was wearing a tuxedo. She was sweet and loved people. When we would go for a walk, she was more interested in the person walking a dog, having no interest in the person's dog itself.

In the year 2008, I ended up having some spine surgery after a nasty fall. She never left my side. We were twenty-four seven for a couple of years. Deciding to sell the home I had lived in for 30 years with my late husband I almost had a nervous breakdown over it. Having her was one of the few consistent and stable things in my life.

After returning to work, I would come home and find her waiting by the door for me. Always happy, wagging her tail, spinning in circles and inevitably bouncing the green ball at my feet. Now was her time, play time with me.

A few years later, on her annual trip to the vet. After some blood work, the vet informed me she had a high liver enzyme count. We would have to keep an eye on it, but they couldn't risk giving her shots for fear of causing complications. So, she became an inside dog but also had her backyard to play in. She remained healthy until the last two years when she was diagnosed with Cushing's Disease. A small tumor was discovered on the pituitary gland which was inoperable. It would eventually wreak havoc with her liver causing an overproduction of cortisone.

I threw myself into finding some homeopathic remedies, including changing her diet to raw dog food, like the wolves and dogs in the wild eat. Some milk thistle, dandelion, and burdock oils all helping with liver defense, and turmeric for inflammation. Jazz loved her new food and eagerly awaited all her meals. Her favorite treat would be some crunchy cheerios. I would drop a couple at a time onto the floor, as she quickly gobbled them up anxiously looking for more.

In November of 2016, when I ended up in the hospital quite unexpectedly for two weeks, I had friends coming over to feed her and play with her, but she was alone at night for the first time. I think she thought I had abandoned her. There was nothing I could do. Upon my return, she was never quite the same. Sleeping on the footstool by my chair, keeping my feet warm, and following me from room to room for fear of losing sight of me.

She started having problems getting herself up. I would have to come and put her on all four legs making sure she had her balance, before letting her walk. At some point, she couldn't get up at all, and she would bark if she lost sight of me, needed water, or wanting to go outside. She still loved her meals and her cheerios, though.

After waking in the morning, I would turn sideways at the foot of the bed and lie next to her, putting my hand on her rubbing her belly and chest for a few minutes, my hand resting on her we would both fall back to sleep for a while. Up for breakfast, our day would start again.

I took her back to the vet, and he suggested we try some pain medicine for a week to see if it would help her. It wasn't the Cushing's Disease but, arthritis in her hips that was preventing her from getting up. She would look up at me her eyes so sad, and her fur was grey and thinning. Her bones are now having trouble supporting her Cushing's belly.

It was time. I set up the appointment with the vet. They brought us into a little room, and I sat with her for a good forty-five minutes saying my good-byes. Tears are welling up and flowing down my cheeks. She looked at me so soulfully, almost like she understood what was happening. The vet came in and asked if I was ready. Yes, I said but are you ever ready for something like this?

"Please tell me I'm doing the right thing," I said.

"You are," he assured me.

I told him I wanted to hold her as he injected the shot that would make her sleepy. She drifted slowly off, peaceful in my arms. Then after came the shot that would stop her heart. It was only a few seconds and, she was gone. No longer in pain.

Entering the house that night, I expected to see her familiar face greeting me, but instead just her blanket on the kitchen floor. I burst into tears, what would I do without her. Every part of me ached. My body felt like someone had hit me with a baseball bat, my eyes almost swollen shut from crying. It was the first time in my life that I could remember not having a pet. I woke several times during the night looking down at the foot of the bed, hoping to see her lying there. Every day since something will remind me of her. When I cleaned the floor, I found a single cheerio under my chair, and I burst into tears again, sobbing hysterically.

She was with me for the most part with the writing of this book. Lying on the footstool, keeping my feet warm. Now the footstool is empty, and a hollow feeling fills my insides. Who will I read my chapters to now? When will the emotional pain cease? It seems that every loss brings up all the other losses that we have had in our lifetime to look at again and grieve some more. It is traumatic. The love of a dog is unconditional. Time will never change that, and I will hold her in my heart forever. My loving and faithful companion.

CONNECTIVITY

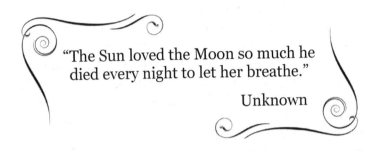

"The Sun loved the Moon so much he died every night to let her breathe."

Unknown

I am back at the window, looking out at the trees. There is a cool breeze blowing. The snow has stopped falling. All is peaceful it seems, sitting in my chair with my blanket wrapped around. I close my eyes and drift off to sleep. Dreaming of my loved ones and wondering when I will see them again. Somehow, I am aware of my feelings in and out of consciousness. Sensing their presence, they are here. They never left really.

I feel pleasantly resigned, accepting that I am right where I am supposed to be. All quiet, connected, not alone. People in my space. I need to release that. Prefer my space. I need to get to that place. I shut out all outside noises so that I can create my reality. Reality is a good word, everything that is and has been, whether it is observable or comprehensible. I need to stay focused at the moment searching for meaning. The words will come easily, effortlessly, and painlessly. Free flowing is bringing me back to self, back to the beginning to what I knew before I entered this world. Calm, no anxiety, no worries.

In writing this book, I have learned so much about myself, which has helped me to move forward in my life. It's been a lesson in trusting the process and, connecting with others, most of them complete strangers. To lose one's self in your imagination is truly the highest form of connectedness to self. Learn to be, to accept, to dream of new heights it's a very simple process that we make all too complicated. Soar with the eagles, fly with the wind in your hair. Connect with self your best companion in good times and in bad. Do something you love, create your reality, believe.

I'm learning to love myself so that I can love others. My journey is a long one, still with much to learn. I'm not done yet; I'm just beginning. A new start, a new life, unlike any I have ever known. I'm excited but quietly not wanting to disturb the peacefulness. Am I lonely? No, not really. I know that I am never alone. That moment when you realize with absolute clarity the infinite and infinitely varied interconnection of all aspects of all universes. I can sense the vibrations and frequencies of light and sound all around me. So, this is where I start my story. At the end.

MY NEW FRIEND

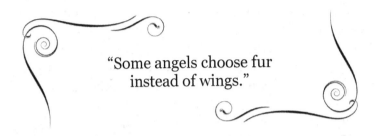

"Some angels choose fur
instead of wings."

Jazz has been gone for about six months now. I continue to work on my manuscript, but the house is ever so quiet now that she is gone. It feels as though a part of my spirit went with her. I decide it's time for a new friend. The search begins. Her name is Izzie, when I go to see her she is very timid and quiet, but as I pick her up, she nuzzles her tiny soft head under my chin and rests there, licking me with her little pink tongue. She has picked me.

Black in color like Jazz with a little white tuft on her chest. Soft and silky she looks like a little-stuffed animal. Homeward bound we are. Izzie is very sweet and playful. Laughter has returned to the house. Her toys are always strewn from one end to the other, and it looks like a two-year-old is living here. She's always bringing me gifts of dried leaves, stones, and sticks, whatever she can drag through the doggy door. She amuses herself as I write, now and then rearing up and giving an endearing little bark when she needs attention.

She gets excited when I open the freezer, as she loves frozen broccoli and peas, devouring them eagerly. When I remove my socks, she quickly snatches one running off with it. Taking it into her pen gently playing with it and never chewing a hole. Occasionally while I'm doing the laundry, a sock will come up missing only to be found somewhere tucked away. She buries her chew bones in the backyard, and when she returns to the house, her nose is usually covered in dirt.

Upon throwing the ball for her whether its down the hallway or outside, she runs and sometimes hops more than a foot in the air in an attempt to retrieve it. I'm beginning to think I should have named her Tigger. While I rest in my chair, she will lie on the footstool or cuddle beside me, demanding some attention. When night comes, I can hear the patter of little paws right behind me as I walk down the hallway. I place Izzie in her pen on the floor beside my bed. She curls up. Lights are turned off. Night, Izzie. All is quiet. I think she is a Joy, as I close my eyes to dream.

C. Lee Roggeman

THE LURE OF THE DRAGONFLY

The lure of the dragonfly has been in existence for over 300 million years, continuing to draw people from many cultures and civilizations. They are a symbol of change and self-realization, navigating the environment with elegance and grace, as they begin life in the water and magically transition to life in the air. Dragonflies are mystical and wonderous, reminding us of the change that can occur with the slightest breeze. They provide the courage and strength to move through illusions and bring dreams into reality, helping us on our path of discovery and enlightenment. They show us that no matter how brief our time here; we are never too old to make this kind of life transitions and transformations.

The spirit of the dragonflies is very powerful. In some Native American beliefs, it is said that the dragonflies are a symbol of renewal after a time of great hardship. The Japanese believe that dragonflies are symbolic of success, victory, happiness, strength, and courage. In Indian culture they believe that dragonflies are the embodiment of spirits that have already gone on; they are the bringers of dreams from the afterlife. When a dragonfly sits on your shoulder, all your dreams are thought to come true. Listen to the wind in your soul with heartfelt anticipation, lightness of being and Joy!

The writing of this book was set in motion by a force far greater than me. It is compelling and written from the heart. Life brings us challenges but also rewards. Sad times but also good ones. Pain is a doorway, through which you can find the magic in a myriad of facets that compose one's life; more importantly, healing from within. Stay positive and focused in the face of adversity. Practice mindfulness and in the silence, find the true nature of yourself.

ABOUT THE AUTHOR

Let me tell you a little bit about myself. I was born and raised in western New York; I was fortunate enough to grow up just minutes from a small town called Lily Dale Assembly. It is the oldest spiritual center in the United States. It was here that my spiritual journey began. My mother would bring me for what is called Summer Session since the winters coming off Lake Erie were so severe that everyone departed until Summer would once again return.

I am a self-taught artist, a gifted painter, ceramicist, mosaic and tile designer with a degree in interior design. I'm a writer with a passion for creativity, and I have a keen interest in the arts. Always reading; you will find that I have four or five books going at the same time. Everything from spiritual, self-help, poetry, romantic travels, and the latest on scientific discoveries. I also enjoy listening to music, cooking, singing, and dancing. I love dogs (all animals really). My newest addition is a seven-month-old puppy named Izzie, who has brought joy back into my world.

Now residing in Arizona and enjoy spending time with my son and daughter-in-law and my three wonderful grandchildren, watching their cheer competitions, baseball, and football games.

Circumstances and synchronicities have all led me on a new journey of creativity in writing. My true reward is to bestow upon my readers a sense of belonging and hope during times of illness, trauma, loss, grief, and sadness. Because at the core of every human existence is survival.